ARTISAN BEER

D0831692

ARTISAN BEER

Gary Monterosso

BURFORD BOOKS

Library of Congress Cataloging-in-Publication Data

Monterosso, Gary.
  Artisan beer / Gary Monterosso.
      p. cm.
  Includes index.
  ISBN 978-1-58080-168-3
  1. Beer. 2. Microbreweries. 3. Beer. I. Title.
  TP577.M65 2011
  663'.42—dc23
                    2011038460

CONTENTS

I

AN INTRODUCTION TO ARTISAN BEER

The renaissance in beer making that started several decades ago had its roots in the brewing centers of the world, a factor noted by the new generation of craftsmen. Flavors and styles were adapted by this group of artisan brewers, often designed to please themselves and their colleagues. No longer would the mass-marketed varieties be adequate; it was time for a change. Beer makers opted to create their own take on how beer should taste and trusted that the public would approve.

These artisan brewers analyzed what was in the market, frequently using non-American beers as their guide. In my talks with brewers, especially those in the midst of building a new beverage, it would not be unusual to see bottles of various beers being sampled and dissected. "What do I like about this?" "How can I accomplish what I want, yet remain true to the style?" were questions asked.

Small test batches were produced and people, often from the general public, provided feedback, much of which was employed in the final recipe. Ultimately, however, the brewer decided for himself the specifics and then produced his beer.

Now, well into the twenty-first century, this new group of artisans has taken the reins. They started as homebrewers, honing their skills on a limited basis to a small but appreciative audience. There are no rules, ingredients vary, and, in some cases, brewers do not replicate the same beer twice. Imagine drinking a Budweiser or Coors that didn't always taste the same! That's part of the beauty of beer today.

I had my first taste of beer before the age of two. That got your attention, didn't it? I'm not petitioning for a guest spot on *Intervention,* nor am I suggesting that I've ever had an issue with alcohol abuse in my family. I can recall my mother having a glass of beer and giving me a sip—much to the amusement to the rest of my family—because I liked the feel of "toam" (that's "foam" to you). I don't think she really liked the stuff that much, but everyone seemed to enjoy my performance whenever a bottle was opened.

Even as a young boy and well shy of legal drinking age, I was able to have a beer at home, under the supervision of my parents. This made me the envy of all the guys in my neighborhood. Friends would tell me how cool my dad was because I was allowed to drink at home.

In reality they had no idea of my parents' logic. My mother and father felt that, under proper supervision, a slight intake of beer would instill respect for the beverage when a child was maturing. Think

Malted barley is grain that is allowed to sprout to a degree before it is dried. This converts starch into simple sugar and enzymes necessary in the brewing process.

of it. Tell a child not to do something and what frequently is the outcome? That kid wants to do what is forbidden. Knock on wood, but overconsumption never was a concern for me. I guess you could call it "love at first sip," but, as you now understand, my love of beer has existed just about as long as I've been alive. And now we are in an era when the choices are broad with flavors to suit all tastes. It is the perfect time to enjoy the most social of all adult beverages, beer.

In its most basic form, beer is made from water, yeast, an herb or spice for flavor, and a malted grain. Although barley normally is that grain, rice, corn, wheat, and other items can also be used.

Evidence exists that barley, a substance that produces good beer but not-so-good bread, was grown six thousand years ago in Mesopotamia. Other cultures, such as that of the Sumerians, have left artifacts that affirm the production of beer. In some societies, beer served as legal tender. The people who built the Egyptian pyramids were given the beverage as payment, known as *kash*. It would be safe to say that the drink was accepted universally throughout the recorded history of humankind.

Credited with being the makers of the first beer, Sumerians, living in what is present day Iraq, created a form of wedge writing on clay tablets sometime around the 4th century B.C. This tablet depicts one of the most important discoveries to the civilization, directions on how to make beer, quite possibly discovered several centuries earlier.

For hundreds of years, beer was perceived as a nutritious concoction, at least in part because the presence of alcohol made it a safer beverage choice than water.

As time progressed, the science of brewing evolved into a deep-rooted native trade, where the drink was made for local consumption. Because transportation consisted of horse-drawn carts traversing bumpy dirt roads, it made little sense to worry about sending beer over long distances. That thought, however, came to an end during the era of exploration to the New World.

Although a maize beer was created by Mexicans, brewing first took place in what would become the colonies in the late 1500s, years before the first settlement at Jamestown. In September 1620, the Pilgrims set sail on the ship *Mayflower* from England. The 102 people on board (only 35 of whom actually sought religious freedom) simply wanted to leave England for a new life in America. The two-thousand-mile voyage took over two months to complete.

Aboard the ship were items such as bread, fruits, dried meats, cheese—and beer. Unusual, you say? Including beer on sea crossings was common practice in the years prior to refrigeration, as fresh water would go bad quickly. (Remember, this was before chlorine and filtered water.) With its alcohol content, beer remained potable longer than water. Additionally, there are records indicating that the Pilgrims landed on the shores of Massachusetts in part because of a lack of beer.

In *Saints and Strangers,* author George F. Willison refers to John Alden as "tall, blond and very powerful in physique . . . a cooper by trade, he was now carefully tending the Pilgrims' precious barrels of beer."

A journal entry from 1622 declared that the Pilgrims actively looked for a place to set up a permanent landing, "our victuals being much spent, especially our beer."

Had there been more beer on the ship, might they have landed on what now is New York? As for the Puritans who set sail for Massachusetts Bay a decade later, Willison wrote that their "good ship *Arbella* carried 10,000 gallons of wine, fourteen tons of fresh water and forty-two tons of beer."

Throughout the seventeenth century, those people who chose to travel to the colonies of Maryland and Virginia faced similar risks: pirates, warships, storms, sickness, and disease. Add to that the sameness of being at sea with no change of surroundings. Conditions were cramped with little headroom, causing people to travel with supplies and much of the ship's cargo. Ventilation was poor. Depending on one's social status, time spent on deck was limited and occurred only when there would be no interference with the sailors who labored on the ship. During times of inclement weather, air hatches were sealed to prevent water from entering. Diseases such as dysentery or typhoid spread quickly.

Food that was brought on board usually was eaten cold, although some of it could be cooked on the ship's hearth, depending upon the size of the vessel. In any event, the same foods were eaten every day.

In ancient Egypt, brewing often was done by women, in part to make extra money. To the left, workers are crumbling lightly baked bread into small pieces before it is strained with water. Fruit was added to provide additional fermentables before the mixture was placed in a large vat, then stored in jars.

Biscuits, known as hardtack, were baked until rock-hard so they might last as long as possible. Before they were eaten, they would be soaked in beer to try to soften them. Why beer and not water? As I mentioned earlier, beer remained safe to drink, whereas water turned bad. It was common practice to use one's teeth to strain water in an effort to remove the algae and bugs that tended to fill the cask after a week.

Make no mistake about it, although beer remained drinkable for much longer than water, it did not have an endless shelf life. The British navy had to cope with long journeys, especially when traveling to warm regions, resulting in flat, spoiled beer. Keep in mind that these primitive brews were unfiltered, suggesting that they were cloudy in appearance. That murkiness came from the presence of yeast, meaning that not having beer usually meant not having the B vitamins that the drink supplied. In addition, the beer was relatively weak, providing just enough alcohol to keep the fresh water from turning undrinkable.

By the mid-1700s, another beverage became popular with sailors: grog. Because colonization had expanded and the men aboard the ships were being sent on longer expeditions, some of which were to balmy climates, grog became the drink of choice. Rum was issued to sailors, but many instances of drunkenness occurred, adversely affecting the operation of the ship. Up to one-quarter of a pint of rum was given twice a day to each person. In time, Admiral Edward Vernon ordered it to be diluted at the rate of one part rum to three parts water. Vernon had the nickname "Old Grogram" because of the grogram coat he wore, and his sailors called the diluted rum grog after the admiral. The term *groggy* originated at this time, an indication of a person who was feeling the effects of drinking a bit too much. The rationing of rum continued in the Royal Navy until 1969.

Sailors stationed in the English Channel maintained their love of beer and were issued a gallon of it daily, per person. The same practice applied to all men stationed in cool climates. The problem of keeping the drink fresh for those long trips into the tropics had to be addressed.

Before the end of the century, the government decided to get involved. A number of ideas were put forth and considered. Finally, a suggestion was made that brewers should boil away most of the wort (pronounced *wert,* this is the liquid prior to fermentation). Then sailors could add water at sea, providing a fresher beverage. Even though this procedure worked well in cool waters, the obstacle relating to warm territories was not overcome. As British troops moved into India, something had to be done, and soon.

To preserve as much freshness as possible, ale was placed in the lower part of the ship's hull, the coolest part of the vessel. Yet the temperature varied greatly. Documents from this time period confirm a range from the low fifties to the mid-eighties, particularly when the ships entered the equatorial regions and also as they approached India. Take a four- or five-month crossing and couple it with temperature extremes and the constant swaying of the boat and you have the ingredients for severely damaging the quality of any beer. Yet brewers continued to make beer for export.

Porter, a dark roasty style of beer that was extremely popular in London, typically was the beer sent to India. Regrettably, it arrived tasting stale and sour. Also, the dark ales plainly were not as satisfying to the colonists now living in the warmth of their new country.

The solution came from a brewer living in London. Until this time, most brewers were trying to alter their methods, in an attempt to turn out a more stable beer. George Hodgson, however, created his India ale, a derivation of his pale ale.

Hodgson's ales were among the first beers that were not brown or black. What separated India ales from all others was the increased alcohol content, a primary weapon against spoilage. Brewers also recognized the preservative qualities that hops offered. Consequently, Hodgson added an additional dose of hops (and more sugar) to keep the yeast functioning during the lengthy voyage. The end result was a bitter, bubbly pale ale that successfully survived the long trip. Hodgson became a folk hero. Within twenty-five years, beer shipments to India increased fivefold.

By 1830, Hodgson controlled the Indian market, although some unethical business methods were employed. Upon hearing that another brewer was preparing pale ale for export, Hodgson flooded the market with his product, effectively lowering the price and removing competition. Then, in following years, he reduced deliveries, thus recovering lost profits from the past.

Success breeds copiers, and there was no shortage of them throughout England. The best came from an area known as Burton-on-Trent, now considered the brewing hub of the country. The secret was in the water, possibly the most overlooked component in the construction of beer. Burton water is high in sulfates, allowing the brewer to vary the amount of hops used. The net result was a strong, flavorful ale that tasted better and had a longer shelf life than that of Hodgson, ultimately leading to his demise.

India pale ale or IPA remained an export-only drink until a ship heading for India was demolished. Its cargo was sold, and Britons were exposed to this beer's existence. It became enormously popular locally and soon spread throughout much of Western Europe. These were powerful beers indeed, approaching 10 percent alcohol by volume. Before the end of the nineteenth century, all that changed and India pale ales became remarkably weaker.

The British government moved from a structure that taxed the raw materials used, to one that was reliant upon the alcohol content of the wort. Hence, watery beers now were produced. As the Industrial Revolution came to be, including the introduction of refrigeration, IPAs fell out of favor, replaced in the colonial trade as the Germans gained recognition with lager beer.

The practice of equating beer with seafaring has been revived by the Global Beer Network, importers of Piraat, a Belgian-made 10.5 percent alcohol-by-volume India pale ale, brewed in the tradition of the type of beer that probably was found on many seventeenth- and eighteenth-century ships.

Mechanical refrigeration was the single most important innovation that changed the brewing industry. It allowed beer to be moved worldwide. The invention of the microscope meant that yeast action could be studied and improved. As the drinkability of the beverage increased, so did the distance that beer could be successfully shipped. Within a few generations, improvements in transportation changed people from hesitant to enthusiastic travelers.

The Joseph Schlitz Brewing Company, was once the largest beer producer in the world. Its signature slogan was "The Beer That Made Milwaukee Famous." Note the reference to the maintenance of good health by regular consumption of Schlitz with its "Sunshine Vitamin D.

Started in 1829, the Yuengling brewery started in Pottsville, PA and holds
the title of "America's Oldest Brewery." Its fans are among the most loyal of
all beer drinkers. Canada's Molson Brewery actually was founded in 1786.
An American court of law sided with Yuengling in its claim that they may
proclaim themselves as the oldest American brewery, citing a belief that U.S.
residents equate the use of the word "America," with "United States."

Beer has been popular in the United States since the country's
inception. There were more breweries in the late nineteenth century
than exist today, but there are different concerns. Obviously, back then
access to a variety of beers was limited because transportation simply
didn't allow for extensive distribution. Consequently, I'll limit any
further discussion regarding beer history to the period from the mid-
1970s forward.

Certain key events that took place in that decade still resound today.
The year 1976 is considered a landmark in American beer history, as it
was in October of that year that the first modern microbrewery, New
Albion Brewing Co. of Sonoma, California, was incorporated. Keep

in mind that the working definition of a *microbrewery* is a company producing up to fifteen thousand barrels (17,600 hectoliters) of beer annually. Today the word *microbrewery* has evolved into *craft brewery*, an independently owned business turning out up to two million barrels of beer a year. Near the end of the 1970s, there were fewer than fifty breweries in the entire country. Contrast that with a hundred years prior, when close to three thousand breweries existed nationwide.

Although New Albion lasted only six years, the wheels were in motion for an increased interest in full-flavored beers, as opposed to the mass-marketed, cookie-cutter beverages that had been the norm.

Also in the late 1970s, two other elements provided direction for this burgeoning industry. A British writer, Michael Jackson, achieved acclaim for his 1977 book, *The World Guide to Beer*, legitimizing the trade and alerting the masses to the fact that the American beer scene was about to change. In October 1978, President Jimmy Carter signed a decree that legalized homebrewing at the federal level. It was this piece of legislation that was the driving force behind authorization to sanction more areas to permit microbreweries. Less than a decade later, a number of western states had their own micros, including the still-thriving Sierra Nevada Brewing Co. of Chico, California. By the way, I would be remiss not to mention the contribution of Fritz Maytag of appliance fame, who took ownership of a failing San Francisco, California, brewery, the Anchor Brewing Co., and transformed it into a classic example of an industry leader. Anchor remains one of the most respected companies in the business.

In the 1980s, a splinter from the micro, the "brewpub," came into being. What distinguished it from a brewery was the fact that food was served in the place where the beer was made. Although the handcrafted beer remained the primary attraction for those who frequented the brewpub, as time progressed emphasis was given to food preparation. Today any good brewpub will feature an extensive array of beers and a bill of fare that complements the house brews. Some brewpubs have received recognition for excellence from prestigious culinary publications.

The trend toward more flavorful drinks—now known by a number of names, including *craft beer* and *boutique beer*—expanded geographically when the Manhattan Brewing Co. became the first brewpub to open in the East, in New York City. One of the brewers there was Garrett Oliver, who later achieved fame as the brewmaster of the Brooklyn Brewery. No one furthered the developing relationship between beer and food more than Oliver, by way of numerous speaking appearances centered on books he authored, especially *The Brewmaster's Table,* an authoritative expression of beer styles and fine cuisine.

Another pioneer in the business was Jim Koch (pronounced *cook*), who in the 1980s decided to carry on his family's tradition by starting the Boston Beer Company, maker of the popular Samuel Adams line of products. With its flagship Samuel Adams Boston Lager, along with other styles emerging, the company expanded from a few thousand barrels a year to over a million.

Make no mistake about it, despite the enormous surge in the popularity of handcrafted brews, sales of the beverages made by the giants of the trade continued to flourish. Well into the 1990s, the "Big Three"—Anheuser-Busch, Coors, and Miller Brewing—produced three of every four domestic beers. In fact, Anheuser-Busch had surpassed the billion mark in cases produced worldwide. Clever advertising promotions perpetuated the image of the "typical" American beer drinker as a male blue-collar worker and a sports devotee. By the end of the century, however, the perception of that drinker had changed somewhat to include men and women, cultural differences, and the like. This shift in attitudes was fueled by an array of books and periodicals on the subject of beer. In short, the consumer had become more educated. Fifteen hundred breweries operated, and all but a couple of dozen were specialty breweries, turning out new flavors and styles. Remember those 1979 figures? Of forty-four breweries, only two could be considered as specialties.

If you think the popularity of these "new" beers, now called boutique or craft, sounded the death knell for the large breweries, nothing could be farther from the truth. The *Brookston Beer Bulletin* published a listing

The final step in brewing is called "mashing" and occurs when hot water is added to ground malt or "grist." The water breaks down the starch within the grain, converting it into fermentable sugars. This process takes place in huge kettles called "mash tuns," as shown at the Coors brewery in Colorado.

of the top fifty breweries based on 2009 sales. To no one's surprise, the top three were Anheuser-Busch, MillerCoors, and Pabst. Clearly, they are doing something very right. To weigh the immense size of A-B, for example, just two of their brands, Bud Light (the best seller in the United States) and Budweiser, are responsible for annually shipping over seventy million barrels of beer worldwide. Contrast that with a company such as O'Fallon Brewery in Missouri. Keeping in mind that most breweries don't distribute outside their immediate area, O'Fallon sends its beers to about a dozen states in its part of the country. Yet the total number of barrels brewed is approximately four thousand annually, the equivalent of about fifty-four thousand cases. And that reflects a 37 percent increase from 2008.

The Miller Brewery, located in Milwaukee, WI. The company had its origin in 1855. The company's peak in popularity was, in part based on the "Champagne of Beers" advertising slogan from years ago.

Too often we hear it said that beer no longer is a "hip" drink. I recall once walking into a brewpub where eight female servers who had finished their shifts were seated at the bar, enjoying a drink. Seven of them had a colorful martini—well, at least the twenty-first-century version of a martini. Only one was drinking beer. I asked them why so few were drinking their company's beverage and the response was that they really didn't consider beer to be in vogue. I then asked what made it so outdated, in their estimation. Answers didn't waver among the women, with most saying that it wasn't colorful enough or was the drink favored by their fathers and they wanted their own style.

Are those valid claims? Although the sample size is small, I've seen this phenomenon repeated elsewhere. So then, if beer isn't dead, is it wounded?

Many of us recall a 2005 Gallup Poll suggesting that wine had tied beer as the adult beverage of choice. I recall many members of the press, as well as non-beer-drinkers, jumped on the story in their quest to back up claims that the popularity of beer was waning. Now, I'll admit that the numbers do show a narrowing of the gap among wine, spirits, and beer. The question is why? I think the gals I spoke with in the brewpub were on target. The wine and spirits people have done a remarkable job of promoting their preferred beverages to prominence.

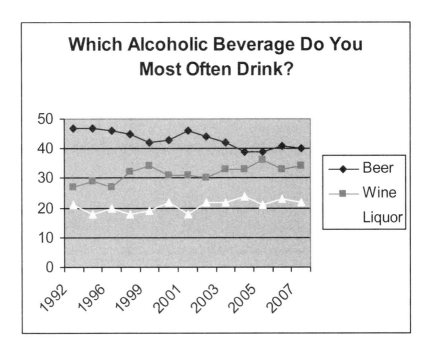

Look at advertisements for these products. They usually reflect some degree of elegance. There's a fancy party or hip club scene attended by beautiful people clad in the latest designer clothing. They are the "beautiful people."

I have to applaud what is going on in the sake world, too. By tradition, the drink is presented in a small wooden box cup called *masu*. I've seen ceramics used, but for the most part you'll see sake served in glass stemware, much the way you'd order wine. Which looks more elegant and more upscale "American"? Yet sake, mistakenly referred to as "rice wine," actually is similar to beer in development. Multiple fermentations takes place; starch is converted to sugar, then the sugar changes to alcohol via the introduction of yeast. Mr. Restaurant Owner, try offering this to your customers in a wooden box and see the looks you'll get. Serve it in a tulip glass and realize how easy it is to get seven dollars.

Compare that with the beer ads that still are common today. You'll see guys sitting around the television on a Sunday afternoon, eating pretzels and chips and pounding down the longnecks by the six-pack. One ad speaks elegance and exclusivity, the other screams commonality. In dealing with a generation of people brought up on upscale merchandise and lifestyle, is it any wonder that they are favoring colorful twenty-first-century Kool-Aid pop "martinis"?

The beer industry should not be held innocent. The gap between the mega- and microbrewers has been just what the rest of the beverage world needed.

What has happened in the last couple of years to swing the numbers back in favor of beer, at least according to the folks at Gallup? It's not in the number of people who call themselves drinkers. In 1945, the percentage of Americans who said they use alcohol was 67 percent. In mid-2007, that number was 64 percent. Gallup did find that young male drinkers prefer beer, but women and older people in general favor wine. The survey indicated that people are drinking more, with the average drinker consuming 4.8 drinks per week as compared with under 4 as recently as 2001.

Over the last few years, there has been an influx of more unusual beer flavors, incorporating atypical ingredients. Take a look at Dogfish Head Brewery as a prime example. At any one time, you'll find beers such as Festina Pêche, a Berliner weisse made with peaches; Chateau Jiahu, an ancient Chinese re-creation using rice flakes, wildflower honey, Muscat grapes, hawthorn fruit, chrysanthemum flowers, and sake yeast;

Fort, a raspberry-infused fruit beer that tops out at 18 percent alcohol by volume (ABV); and Midas Touch Golden Elixir, a hybrid based on the funerary feast of King Midas: elements of barley (beer), Muscat grapes (wine), and honey (mead). To top things off, saffron, one of the most expensive spices in the world, is added to the mix. You don't think the introduction of those beers didn't excite beer drinkers? As esoteric as Dogfish Head is, what they are doing is being replicated at small breweries throughout the country. I once asked a brewer why he was experimenting with bizarre ingredients in his recipes. He said, "I'm small. I'll always remain small. I can afford to take chances and, quite frankly, my customers like it."

Perhaps not so coincidentally, the upsurge in regular drinking has coincided with medical reports suggesting that not only is moderate drinking harmless, but it may also have health benefits. Initially, red wine consumption was linked with heart protection, but more recently that has extended to beer.

According to the Brewers Association, moderate beer consumption (no more than two drinks a day for men, one for women) may be able to:

- Lower rates of heart disease by 30 to 60 percent.
- Aid in bone formation. Beer contains silicon, a mineral that helps to build bone mass.
- Prevent cell damage that can lead to cancer and heart disease. Two ingredients in beer, hops and malt, supply much-needed antioxidants, known to fight disease. Beer contains polyphenols, also found in berries, tea, grapes, wine, olive oil, cocoa, certain nuts, and other fruits and vegetables.
- Reduce incidence of diabetes.
- Protect against certain types of strokes, Alzheimer's disease, and dementia.

Lastly, beer contains no fat or cholesterol. The calories come principally from the alcohol.

As with most things in this world, the key is moderation. If taking a one-hundred-milligram tablet of vitamin E is good, would ingesting fifty times that amount be fifty times better? Because vitamin E acts as an anticoagulant that could lead to bleeding, drastically increasing the dosage is foolish. Likewise, having a couple of bottles of beer a day may have the previously mentioned positives, but multiplying one's intake radically will cause health problems and probably won't do much to guarantee the longevity of your job or marriage.

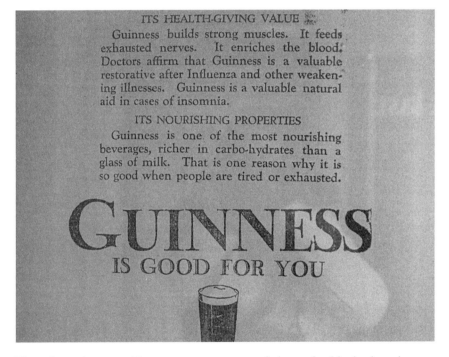

ITS HEALTH-GIVING VALUE
Guinness builds strong muscles. It feeds exhausted nerves. It enriches the blood. Doctors affirm that Guinness is a valuable restorative after Influenza and other weakening illnesses. Guinness is a valuable natural aid in cases of insomnia.

ITS NOURISHING PROPERTIES
Guinness is one of the most nourishing beverages, richer in carbo-hydrates than a glass of milk. That is one reason why it is so good when people are tired or exhausted.

GUINNESS
IS GOOD FOR YOU

Throughout the years, Guinness was recommended as a health drink and researchers have found antioxidant compounds, similar to those in wine and chocolate. For some time, pregnant women were advised to have an occasional glass of it. The company and its American importer make no such claims and allow the flavor and popularity of the drink to speak for itself.

2

BEER STYLES: ALES, LAGERS, AND HYBRIDS

Most beers fall into one of two principal classifications: ales and lagers. There's a third grouping, small in number, which will be discussed later. Pour a beer and by appearance alone, you'd be hard-pressed to identify its category. What separates ales from lagers is in how they were created. Some companies like to refer to a "born on" date, but I'll leave that to them.

There are complicated, esoteric descriptions of how ales and lagers differ, so let's take the mystery out of it. Simply stated, the key is in the type of yeast used in the fermentation process. Ale yeast does its work under warm conditions, probably not below fifty-five or sixty degrees Fahrenheit and up to about eighty degrees. They tend to do their job at the upper part of the fermentation vessel; thus, ales are known as a "top-fermenting" beverage. Ales are especially popular with microbrewers and homebrewers because they can be consumed within days of packaging. Let's face it, when you own a very small company, who has the time to allow the beer to age? Time is money.

Lagered beers take their name from the German word meaning "to store." Whereas ale yeast likes warmth and the top of the fermenter, lagers are the opposite. Optimum production from most lager yeast strains ranges from roughly thirty-five to sixty degrees. They settle to the bottom of the vat to do their thing.

The time spent in fermentation for ales and lagers is similar. Within a couple of weeks, the resulting liquid can be called beer.

Ah, but here is where the lagering comes into play. For those brews, a move to cold storage takes place, generally for a few weeks. Czechvar, a delightful Czech beer, boasts of a lagering period of ninety days for their premium original lager and up to two hundred days for their specialty beer.

I referred to a third style earlier. For lack of a better term, beers of this variety are called hybrids. Think of the auto industry for comparison. Most of the hybrid cars currently on the market operate based on the combination of gasoline and electric power. In the beer world, hybrids really aren't lagers or ales. Obviously, very few beers qualify for this special distinction. One that does, however, is the immensely popular Anchor Steam, made by Anchor Brewing of San Francisco. Known by the tag *California common*, Anchor Steam is brewed using a special lager yeast. Prior to refrigeration, makers of this style used huge shallow open fermenters that allowed the beer to cool in the chilly Bay Area temperatures. The outcome is a malty (somewhat sweet) beer that retains lager's characteristic dryness. Interestingly, this is one of the very few styles that didn't begin in Europe. Be advised that Anchor is not the only brewery making California common beer, although the name *Steam Beer* is trademarked. Old Scratch Amber Lager by Flying Dog Brewery, based in Denver, Colorado, is outstanding and should be readily available in most locations. Also, I've seen plenty of brewpubs that have released their own versions of this beer, but I've yet to sample any as good as the two I've mentioned.

There are other examples of hybrids on the market, and opinions vary as to what constitutes beers of this style. Some feel that the use of fruits or herbs is grounds for reclassification, but stick to the use of either lager or ale yeasts in a nontraditional brewing method.

ALE VERSUS LAGER

Okay, we've gotten the background we need in ales, lagers, and hybrids, but what we still need is a way to generalize about the flavor differences among them. And from here forward, we'll drop hybrids and just focus on the other two.

The manner in which certain strains of yeast work is what sets apart the two primary beer types. Ale yeasts, fermenting at a warmer temperature than lager yeasts, give off esters, those fruity and spicy flavor qualities so prevalent in beers of this sort. Some say ales are more complex than lagers, and I suppose there is truth in that statement. What it means is that the drinker may note a combination of aromas and flavors in those beers. Not all flavors present themselves with the initial sip, either. One sensation may be noted initially, whereas another may come forward later.

Lagers are more straightforward in presentation. Remember, lagered beers are aged for a much longer period than are ales. What maturation does is to deliver evenness. Allowing the beer to rest at chilly temperatures triggers fewer esters than with ales. Consequently, other flavors tend to emerge, including hop bitterness.

There are drinkers who find lagers to be dull and boring. I suspect they've never tasted all-malt lagers, those beers that don't have cereal adjuncts added. A true lager, minus the cheap additions, offers a big malt presence, balanced by a hop bitterness that produces a memorable beverage.

Needless to say, one can find virtually anything on the Internet, including information about beer styles. As with virtually every subject, there's good to be found by Googling, and there's garbage. Depending on your source, you may find anywhere from a few dozen to well over a hundred different classifications of beer. As of 2011, the Brewers Association, hosts of The Great American Beer Festival held each fall in Denver, has identified seventy-nine types. The World Beer Cup, a spring event, shows ninety. Whatever you accept as true is immaterial for our purpose here. Frankly, many of the varieties are so esoteric, you simply won't find them in most well-stocked packaged goods stores. Vendors are in business to make money, and they tend to carry the best-selling styles. That's what our focus is. I'll identify the most common types of beer along with representative samples of each, then let you find them and begin your enjoyment.

I am going to mention a book that is invaluable for beer research. Michael Kuderka is the author of *The Essential Reference of Domestic Brewers and Their Bottled Brands,* published by MC Basset, LLC, in Asbury, New Jersey. Michael decided to write his book after going to a beer festival and then realizing he didn't necessarily know where to go to purchase the beers he enjoyed. Hasn't that happened many times over? At New Jersey's Atlantic City Beer Festival, only beers that are readily accessible to the public are invited to attend as vendors. Promoters insist that company representatives be present to answer questions from those curious patrons who might require additional information.

Kuderka's book is a reference, and that might turn off some people. However, if you are looking for information on beer styles and availability, as well as a complete brewery portfolio, there is no better reference to be had anywhere. When I was a regular on a program on the Sirius Satellite Radio network, Kuderka did a guest spot, and he was informative and entertaining.

The Beverage Testing Institute, founded in 1981, is a highly respected company that offers unbiased appraisals of wine, spirits, and beer. Based in Chicago, the organization publishes a monthly newsletter called *eTastings* and hosts a free website at Tastings.com. Their expertise goes beyond a mere identification of beer types; rather, they offer commonsense tips dealing with matching beer with food, glassware, and how beer is made. Furthermore, you can search for a beverage of your choosing and read what their team of experts has to report.

Below is a list of the most common beer styles you are likely to find, along with representative brands, created in conjunction with the Beverage Testing Institute.

ALES

Abbey Ales (Dubbel, Tripel, Singel), Trappist Ale

Monastic or abbey ales are an ancient tradition in Belgium in much the same manner as wine production was once closely associated with monastic life in ancient France. Currently, very few working monasteries brew beer within the order, but many have licensed the production of beers bearing their abbey name to large commercial brewers. These abbey ales can vary enormously in specific character, but most are quite strong in alcoholic content, ranging from 6 percent alcohol by volume (ABV) to as high as 10 percent. Generally, abbey ales are labeled as either dubbel or tripel, though this is not a convention that is slavishly adhered to. The former conventionally denotes a relatively less alcoholic and often darker beer, while the latter can often be lighter or blond in color and have a syrupy, alcoholic mouthfeel that invites sipping, not rapid drinking. The lowest-gravity abbey ale in a Belgian brewer's range will conventionally be referred to as a singel, though it is rarely labeled as such.

Trappist ales may only come from seven abbeys of the Trappist order that still brew beer on their premises. Six are in Belgium and one, La Trappe, in Holland. Although the styles may differ widely among them, they all share a common traits of being top-fermented, strong, bottle-conditioned, complex, and fully flavored brews. At most, each abbey produces three different varieties of increasing gravity. These can often improve with some years of cellaring. The ales from Trappist abbeys are: Chimay, Rochefort, Orval, Westmalle, Westvleteren, Achel, and La Trappe. Trappist ales are among the most complex and old-fashioned of beers that you can find. It's little wonder that many connoisseurs treat them as the holy grail of beer drinking.

Among the best: Ommegang, Maredsous 10, Chimay Première, Chimay Grand Reserve, Westmalle Dubbel, Westmalle Tripel, Rochefort 8, Rochefort 10, Westvleteren 12, Orval

Alt

Put simply, an altbier has the smoothness of a classic lager with the flavors of an ale. A more rigorous definition must take account of history. Ale brewing in Germany predates the now predominant lager production. As the lager process spread from Bohemia, some brewers retained the top-fermenting ale process but adopted the cold maturation associated with lager—hence the name Old Beer (*alt* means "old" in German). Altbier is associated with Dusseldorf, Munster, and Hanover. This style of ale is light- to medium-bodied when compared with traditional English ales. In the United States, some amber ales are actually in the alt style.

Among the best: Uerige Sticke, Long Trail Double Bag, Otter Creek Copper Ale

Amber Ales

Many North American brewers are now producing ales that are known as amber ales. This is a more modern, nontraditional style, and many of these beers borrow heavily from the characteristics associated with more classical styles such as pale ales or bitters. Amber ales are light- to medium-bodied and can be anywhere from light copper to light brown in hue. Flavorwise, they can vary from generic and quaffable to serious craft-brewed styles with extravagant hoppy aromas and full malt character. Typically, amber ales are quite malty but not heavily caramelized in flavor. For our purposes, amber ales will also include ales commonly identified as red ales and American ales as, from the consumer's viewpoint, the dividing line between these styles can often be a more a marketing concern than a consistently observed brewing convention.

Among the best: Anderson Valley Boont Amber Ale, Tröegs Hopback Amber Ale, Rogue American Amber Ale, Stone Levitation Ale

American Pale Ale

These brews are golden to light copper in color with a more subtle overall character and lighter body than typical pale ales. English ale fruitiness will probably not be observed. However, the most important criteria are that they are brewed domestically and will have less body and hop and malt character than a pale ale from the same brewery.

Among the best: Sierra Nevada Pale Ale, Anchor Liberty Ale, Otter Creek Pale Ale, Dale's Pale Ale

Barleywine

Barleywine is the evocative name coined by British brewers to describe extremely potent ales that can range from golden copper to dark brown in color. They are characterized by extravagant caramel malt flavors and bittering hops that prevent the malt sweetness from cloying. Rich and viscous, they can have in their most complex manifestations winey flavor profiles with a hint of sweetness. Some examples are vintage-dated and can improve with extended bottle age. These powerful brews are classically sold in small "nip" bottles and can be consumed after dinner or with dessert. The style has become popular among US craft brewers, who often produce them as winter specialties. American versions tend to be a bit hoppier than their British counterparts.

Among the best: Sierra Nevada Bigfoot, Weyerbacher Blithering Idiot, Rogue Old Crustacean, Victory Old Horizontal

Belgian-Style Golden Ale

Belgian golden ales are pale to golden in color with a lightish body for their deceptive alcoholic punch, as much as 9 percent alcohol by volume. Typically such brews undergo three fermentations, the final one being in the bottle, resulting in fine champagne-like carbonation and a huge rocky white head when they are poured. Often such beers can be cellared for six months to a year to gain roundness. These beers are probably best served chilled to minimize the alcoholic mouthfeel.

Among the best: Leffe Blond, Val-Dieu Blond, Affligem Blond

Belgian-Style Strong Ale

Beers listed in this category will generally pack a considerable alcohol punch and should be approached much like you would a barleywine. Indeed, some of them could be considered Belgian-style barleywines. Expect a fruity Belgian yeast character and a degree of sweetness coupled with a viscous mouthfeel.

Among the best: Duvel, Unibroue La Fin du Monde, Allagash Grand Cru, La Chouffe, Brooklyn Local 1

Belgian-Style Red Ale

These are also known as soured beers, and their defining character classically comes from having been aged for some years in well-used large wooden tuns, allowing bacterial action in the beer and thus imparting the sharp "sour" taste. Hops do not play much role in the flavor profile of these beers, but whole cherries can be macerated with the young beer to produce a cherry-flavored Belgian red ale. These styles are almost exclusively linked to one producer in northern Belgium, Rodenbach. These ales are among the most distinctive and refreshing to be found anywhere.

Among the best: Rodenbach Grand Cru, Duchesse de Bourgogne, Ommegang Rouge

Belgian-Style Amber Ale

This is not a classic style but nonetheless encapsulates various beers of a similar Belgian theme that do not fit into the more classic mold. Expect amber-hued, fruity, and moderately strong ales (6 percent alcohol by volume) with a yeasty character.

Among the best: New Belgium Fat Tire Amber Ale, Ommegang Rare Vos

Belgian-Style Blonde Ale

This is not a classic style of Belgian ale, but covers the more commercially minded Belgian ales that are lighter in color and moderate in body and alcoholic strength. Fruity Belgian yeast character and mild hopping should be expected.

Among the best: Val-Dieu Blond, Leffe Blonde, Affligem Blond

Biere de Garde

Biere de garde is a Flemish and northern French specialty ale generally packaged distinctively in 750ml bottles with a cork. Historically, the style was brewed as a farmhouse specialty in February and March, to be consumed in the summer months when the warmer weather didn't permit brewing. Typically produced with a malt accent, this is a strong (often over 6 percent) yet delicate bottle-conditioned beer. These brews tend to be profoundly aromatic and are an excellent companion to hearty foods.

Among the best: 3 Monts Grande Réserve Spécial Ale, Perdition, Southampton Biere de Mars

Bitter

Bitter is an English specialty and very much an English term, generally denoting the standard ale, the "session" beer. Bitters are characterized by a fruitiness, light to medium body, and an accent on hop aromas more than hop bitters. Colors range from golden to copper. Despite the name they are not particularly bitter. Indeed, British brewed "bitters" will often be less bitter than US craft-brewed amber ales. A fuller-bodied bitter is labeled as extra special bitter (ESB). These weightier versions of bitter often stand up better to the rigors of travel overseas than the lower-gravity standard versions. An important element of faithful bitters is the English yeast cultures used in fermentation. These impart a fruity, mildly estery character that should be noted in examples of the style. Bitters are now widely emulated in North America, sometimes with domestically grown hops imparting a rather more assertive character than seen in traditional English bitters.

Among the best: Fuller's London Pride, Fuller's ESB, Rogue Younger's Special Bitter

Brown Ale

The precise definition of a brown ale would depend on where you live. In England, it is nowadays much more closely associated with northern England, specifically Tadcaster and Newcastle. These medium-bodied reddish brown beers are malt accented with a nutty character, a gentle fruitiness, and low bitterness. Alcohol is moderate, a maximum of 5 percent ABV. The less prevalent southern English variety, not seen abroad, is much darker in color, sweeter on the palate, and made in a lighter style. English-style brown ales of the former type have become very popular with US brewers, no doubt for the same reason they took hold in England: They offer great drinkability.

Among the best: Newcastle Brown Ale, Samuel Smith's Nut Brown Ale, Smuttynose Old Brown Dog Ale

Dry Stout

Dry stout is closely associated with Ireland. These brews tend to be rich and dark with a definitive bitter note and a drying palate feel. They are classically paired with oysters, although any Irish stout drinker will tell you that a pint it is a meal in itself. Draught (draft) Irish stout is nitrogen-flushed to give it a telltale white creamy head. This process is also effected in cans and bottles with a nitrogen "widget." The style is widely emulated throughout the world and is particularly popular with US microbrewers and brewpubs, often as a more full-bodied and drier interpretation.

Among the best: Guinness Foreign Extra Stout, Lion Stout, Beamish Stout, Rogue Shakespeare Stout

Dunkel/Dark Wheat

Dark wheat beers derive their character from the use of darker malts in the nonwheat ingredients, so that a richer, darker-colored beer can be achieved, along with fuller malt flavors. Dunkel weizens still display the floral, estery qualities of a pale weizen. Dark weizens are produced with or without a secondary fermentation in the bottle, with the corollary that these styles can be yeast sedimented or unsedimented depending upon the preference of the brewer.

Among the best: Franziskaner Hefe-Weisse Dunkel, Weihenstephaner Hefeweissbier Dunkel, Ramstein Classic

Flavored Porter

Flavoring traditional beer styles is a particular feature of the creative US craft-brewing scene. Flavorings used in porters are typically dark berry fruits and coffee. When skillfully done, the effect can be greater than the sum of its parts.

Among the best: Old Engine Oil, Samuel Adams Honey Porter, Fuller's London Porter

Flavored Stout

Flavored stouts still are stouts, be they sweeter or drier. Dark fruits, coffee, and chocolate are particularly popular, and the marriage of flavors can turn this style into one that pleases even those who don't favor dark beers.

Among the best: Young's Double Chocolate Stout, Samuel Adams Cream Stout, Left Hand Milk Stout

Flemish-Style Brown Ale

These are complex dark beers most closely associated with the town of Oudenaarde in Flanders. The authentic examples are medium- to full-bodied beers that are influenced by a number of factors: high bicarbonate in the brewing water to give a frothy texture; a complex mix of yeasts and malts; blending of aged beers; and aging in the bottle before release. In the best examples, the flavor profile is reminiscent of olives, raisins, and brown spices and could be described as "sweet and sour." These beers are not hop-accented and are of low bitterness.

Among the best: Liefmans Goudenband, Petrus Old Brown

Hefeweizen

Weizen bier is a top-fermenting beer style that originates from southern Germany, particularly Bavaria and is brewed with at least 50 percent wheat in the mash. Hefeweizens are refreshing, highly carbonated beers ideal for quenching summer thirsts. They undergo secondary fermentation, often in the bottle, and the yeast strains used for this purpose impart a spicy, clove-like flavor. *Hefe* (the German word for "yeast") on the label denotes that the bottle contains yeast sediment. Alcohol content is typically 5 to 5.5 percent ABV, giving these beers a medium to medium-full body. Hop flavors play a very insignificant role in the flavor profile. The best examples to be found are still authentic Bavarian imports, although some good domestic examples are produced and are often available as a draft option.

Among the best: Tröegs Dreamweaver Wheat, Hacker-Pschorr Weisse, Schneider Weisse

Imperial Stout

Imperial stout is an extra-strong version of stout that was originally brewed by the British to withstand the rigors of export to Russia and the Baltic states. This style is dense, opaque black and strong in alcohol

(6 to 7 percent) with a note of sweetness. Burnt cocoa and dried fruit flavors are typical. Russian Imperial stouts originate from recipes that British brewers tailored to the tastes of the Imperial Russian court. Imperial stout was almost extinct until re-created by the British brewer Samuel Smiths in the early 1980s. The style has now been embraced by US craft brewers as a winter specialty.

Among the best: Rogue Russian Imperial Stout, Dogfish Head World Wide Stout, Brooklyn Black Chocolate Stout, Victory Storm King, Weyerbacher Heresy

India Pale Ale (IPA)

These beers are deep gold to amber in color and are usually characterized by floral hop aromas and a distinctive hop bitterness on the finish. IPAs were originally brewed by British brewers in the nineteenth century, when British troops and colonizers depended upon supplies of beer shipped from England. Standard ales did not survive the journey, so brewers developed high-gravity, highly hopped ales that withstood shipment in casks to their largest market, India. This style, probably not anywhere near as bitter as it was when destined for India, continues to be brewed in a toned-down manner in the UK and is undergoing a mini revival at present. However, US craft brewers have claimed the style as their own, and often brew them with assertive Pacific Northwest hop varieties that give such examples a hugely aromatic hop accent.

Among the best: Smuttynose IPA, Magic Hat Blind Faith, Samuel Smith's India Ale, Brooklyn East India Pale Ale

Irish Ale

Irish ales are characterized by their reddish color, malt accents, slightly sweet palate, and low hopping. If true to style, they are not overly bitter, reflecting on the historical fact that the Irish have never taken to huge amounts of hops in their traditional beers. In their native land, Irish ales have long played second fiddle to stouts and prior to that, porters.

Lacking a truly indigenous character, many versions being revived in the United States owe more to Celtic marketing than to a distinct character, although the color and high drinkability are the usual reference points.

Among the best: Smithwick's Ale, Beamish Red

Kölsch

Kölsch is a style emanating from Cologne in Germany. In Germany (and the European community), the term is strictly legally limited to the beers from within the city environs of Cologne. Simply put, Kölsch has the color of a pilsner with some of the fruity character of an ale. This is achieved with the use of top-fermenting yeasts and pale Pilsner malts. The hops are accented on the finish, which classically is dry and herbal. It is a medium- to light-bodied beer and delicate in style.

Among the best (US versions): Goose Island Summertime Kölsch, Victory Kölsch Ale, Geary's Summer Ale

Kristall Weizen

A kristall weizen is a filtered weizen ale. *Kristall* on the label of a weizen specifically denotes that a weizen has been filtered prior to bottling to remove the protein haze and yeast often suspended in such beers. Kristall weizens lack the yeasty and spicy complexity often associated with hefeweizen beers and have a cleaner and more delicate flavor. Floral, fruity aromas are often noted in classic examples of this style, though healthy alcohol content of 5 to 5.5 percent ABV will give a medium- to medium-full-bodied character.

Among the best: Weihenstephaner Kristallweissbier, Tucher Kristall Weizen

Lambics

Gueuze, fruit lambic, faro: Lambic beers are perhaps the most individualistic style of beer in the world. Lambics are produced in tiny quantities immediately south of the Belgian capital, Brussels. Lambic brewers use native wild yeasts in the open-air fermentation process to produce these specialties. This unusual fermentation, in conjunction with extended aging in ancient oak barrels, imparts a unique vinous character with a refreshing sourness and astonishing complexity. Lambics labeled as gueuze are a blend of young and old beers. Such blending results in a sharp champagne-like effervescence and tart, toasty flavors. Those labeled as faro have had sugar, caramel, or molasses added in order to impart a note of sweetness. Lambic beers, however, are more often seen in the United States when they have been flavored with fruits. *Kriek* (cherry) and *framboise* (raspberry) are the most popular and traditional fruits employed. Other exotic fruits are widely used in juice form in the more commercial examples of lambic beer, much to the consternation of purist connoisseurs.

Among the best: Lindemans Framboise, Lindemans Kriek, Lindemans Pêche, Boon Kriek, Cantillon Rosé de Gambrinus

Mild Ale

Mild ale is a traditional style of English ale characterized by a color ranging from golden to dark, a sweet malt flavor, and subtle hopping levels, all within a low-alcohol frame. Its purpose is to allow the drinker to get a full quotient of flavor in a "session" beer, a trick to which English ale brewing lends itself readily. In the 1940s, mild was more popular than bitter in English pubs, though it is less common now. US craft brewers occasionally pay homage to this style.

Among the best: Coopers Dark Ale, Harpoon Brown Session Ale

Oatmeal Stout

This brew is a variation on a sweet stout, with a small proportion of oats used in place of roasted malt, producing an enhanced body and mouthfeel. This flavor originally was brewed by the British when stouts were thought of as a nutritious part of an everyday diet. After having fallen from favor, the style was revived by Yorkshire brewer Samuel Smith in 1980. They tend to be highly flavorful with a velvety texture and sometimes a hint of sweetness. Oatmeal stouts are now a very popular staple of the US craft-brewing scene.

Among the best: Samuel Smith's Oatmeal Stout, Wolaver's Oatmeal Stout, Young's Oatmeal Stout

Porter

Porters are reddish brown to black in color, medium- to medium-full-bodied, and characterized by a flavor profile that can vary from very subtle dark malts to fully roasted, smoky flavors. Because this is a centuries-old style, there are differences of opinion with regard to what a true porter was actually like and there can be wide variations from one brewer's interpretation to the next. Roasted malt should provide the flavoring character, rather than roasted barley as is used with stouts. Stronger, darker versions and lighter more delicate versions are equally valid manifestations of the style. The influence of hops can often be notable in the richer craft-brewed examples of the style. Although porter was the drink of the masses of the 1700s London, it is not a significant factor in the British market today, despite the production of a few outstanding English examples. In the United States, it is enjoying newfound popularity among craft brewers, and many fine examples are produced.

Among the best: Fuller's London Porter, Anchor Porter, Sierra Nevada Porter, Alaskan Smoked

Saison

Saison beers are distinctive specialty beers from the Belgian province of Hainuat. These beers were originally brewed in the early spring for summer consumption, though contemporary Belgian saisons are brewed all year round with pale malts and well dosed with English and Belgian hop varieties. Lively carbonation ensues from a secondary fermentation in the bottle. The color is classically golden orange, and the flavors are refreshing with citrus and fruity hop notes. Sadly, these beers are underappreciated in their home country, and their production is limited to a small number of artisanal producers who keep this style alive. With a typically hoppy character, the saison is an extremely esoteric style that should appeal to any devotee of craft beers. Fortunately, there does seem to be a revival of this style among brewers in the United States.

Among the best: Hennepin, Saison Dupont, Foret

Scottish Ale

Scottish ales are typically full-bodied and malty, with some of the classic examples being dark brown in color. They are more lowly hopped than the English counterparts and often have a slightly viscous and sweet caramel malt character due to incomplete fermentation. Scottish-style ales can be found in far-flung corners of the world, where faithful versions are brewed—a legacy of its popularity in the British Empire. In the United States, many craft brewers produce a Scottish-style ale. The "export" versions produced by Scottish brewers—the type most often encountered in the US—are considerably stronger and maltier than the standard versions made available to Scottish beer drinkers.

Among the best: Samuel Adams Scotch Ale, Belhaven Scottish Ale, Robert the Bruce Scottish Ale

Strong Ale

Strong ales are sometimes referred to as old ales, stock ales, or winter warmers. These beers are higher-alcohol versions (typically between 5.5 to 7.5 percent ABV) of pale ales, though not as robust or alcoholic as barleywines. Usually a deep amber color, these brews generally have a sweet malty palate and a degree of fruitiness. If bottle-conditioned, strong ales can improve for some years in the bottle, in some cases eventually obtaining sherry-like notes.

Among the best: Fuller's 1845, Avery Old Jubilation, Gale's Prize Old Ale, Samuel Adams Utopias

Sweet Stout

Sweet stouts are largely a British specialty. These stouts have a distinctive sweetness to the palate and often show chocolate and caramel flavors. They are sometimes known as milk or cream stouts. These beers obtain their characters by using chocolate malts and lactic (milk) sugars in the brewing process.

Among the best: Young's Double Chocolate Stout, Lancaster Milk Stout, Marston's Oyster Stout, Left Hand Milk Stout

Weizen Bock

Weizen bocks are essentially winter wheat beers, originally brewed in Bavaria. The color can be pale gold to brown. They are of higher alcoholic strength, as high as 7 percent ABV, showing a warming personality, though they should still have a significant "rocky" head when poured. These beers combine the character of hefeweizens and doppelbocks and as such are rich and malty with estery, yeasty qualities. They show a note of wheaty crispness through the finish.

Among the best: Schneider Aventinus, Ramstein Winter Wheat, Victory Moonglow Weizenbock

Wheat Ale

As the name would suggest, these are ales that use a proportion of wheat in the mash to add a protein haze. Wheat ales, inspired by the German weizen tradition, were popular before Prohibition in the United States and are enjoying a resurgence in popularity. This generic category encapsulates the diverse interpretation of the classic German weizen styles brewed in America and elsewhere. A host of variables ranging from the wheat/malt ratio, hopping, and filtration/nonfiltration all contribute to wide variations on the theme. Generally, US examples feature a more marked hop accent than classic German weizen styles and are often drier.

Among the best: Lancaster Strawberry Wheat, Sweaty Betty Blonde, Circus Boy

White/Wit Beer

Wit beer is a style of unfiltered wheat beer. It is distinctly Belgian in origin and is still very closely associated with this lowland country. Wits employ a proportion of unmalted wheat in the mash but also have flavor added in the form of curaçao, orange peel, and coriander, among other ingredients. Their appearance is marked by a hazy white precipitate, and these beers generally have some sedimentation. Typically these are very refreshing summer thirst quenchers. They are not widely produced in the United States, but some notable examples can be found.

Among the best: Hoegaarden Original White Beer, Allagash White, Unibroue Blanche de Chambly, Blue Moon Belgian White

Winter Ales

Spiced winter ales are popular among US craft brewers. Typically, they are strong ales that have had some spice added during the brewing process. True to their name, they make ideal sipping beers with which to ward off winter's chill and get a dose of seasonal spices. This style is usually brewed before Christmas, and brewers frequently make annual adjustments to their often secret recipes in an effort to obtain that perfect symbiosis among spices, hops, and malt.

Among the best: Samuel Adams Old Fezziwig Ale, Anchor Our Special Ale, Samuel Smith's Winter Welcome Ale, Jubelale

LAGERS

Amber Lagers

Amber is a vaguely defined style of lager much favored by US lager brewers. It's darker in color, anywhere from amber- to copper-hued, and generally more fully flavored than a standard pale lager. Caramel malt flavors are typical, and hopping levels vary considerably from one brewery to the next, though they are frequently hoppier than the true Vienna lager styles on which they are loosely based. Alcohol levels are generally a maximum of 5 percent ABV.

Among the best: Blue Point Toasted Lager, Abita Amber, Samuel Adams Boston Lager, Brooklyn Lager

Black/Schwarz Beer

Originally brewed in Thuringia, a state in eastern Germany, these lager-style brews were known to be darker in color than their Munich counterparts. Often relatively full-bodied and rarely under 5 percent ABV, these beers classically feature a bitter chocolate, roasted malt note, and rounded character. Hop accents are generally low. This obscure style was picked up by Japanese brewers and is made in small quantities there. Schwarz beers are not often attempted by US craft brewers.

Among the best: Samuel Adams Black Lager, Saranac Black Forest, Bohemian Black Lager

Bock

Bocks are a specific type of strong lager historically associated with Germany and specifically the town of Einbeck. These beers range in color from pale to deep amber tones and feature a decided sweetness on the palate. Bock styles are an exposition of malty sweetness that is classically associated with the character and flavor of Bavarian malt. Alcohol levels are quite potent, typically 6 to 7 percent ABV. Hop aromas are generally low, though hop bitterness can serve as a balancing factor against the malt sweetness. Many of these beers' names or labels feature some reference to a goat. This is a play on words in that the word *bock* also refers to a male goat in the German language. Many brewers choose to craft these beers for consumption in the spring (often called maibock) or winter, when their warmth can be fully appreciated.

Among the best: Spoetzl Shiner Bock, Samuel Adams Chocolate Bock, 1888 Bock

Dark/Dunkel Lager

Dunkel is the original style of lager, serving as the forerunner to the pale lagers of today. They originated in and around Bavaria, and are widely brewed both there and around the world. This is often what average consumers are referring to when they speak of dark beer. At their best, these beers combine the dryish chocolate or licorice notes associated with the use of dark roasted malts and the roundness and crisp character of a lager. Examples brewed in and around Munich tend to be a little fuller-bodied and sometimes have a hint of bready sweetness to the palate, a characteristic of the typical Bavarian malts used.

Among the best: Ayinger Altbairisch Dunkel, Negra Modelo, Spaten Dunkel

Doppelbock

This is a subcategory of the bock style. Doppelbocks are extra strong, rich, and weighty lagers characterized by an intense malty sweetness with a note of hop bitterness to balance the sweetness. Color can vary from full amber to dark brown, and alcohol levels are potently high, typically 7 to 8 percent ABV. Doppelbocks were first brewed by the Paulaner monks in Munich. At the time, they were intended to be consumed as "liquid bread" during Lent. Most Bavarian examples end in the suffix *–ator,* in deference to the first commercial example, which was named Salvator (savior) by the Paulaner brewers.

Among the best: Ayinger Celebrator, Samiclaus Bier, Spaten Optimator

Dortmunder Export

Well balanced, smooth, and refreshing, Dortmunders tend to be stronger and fuller than other pale lagers or Munich Helles styles. They may also be a shade darker and a touch hoppier. The style originates from the city of Dortmund in northern Germany. Dortmunder export came about during the Industrial Revolution, when Dortmund was the center of the coal and steel industries, and the swelling population needed a hearty and sustaining brew. The *export* appendage refers to the fact that Dortmunder beers were "exported" to surrounding regions. Today the term *Dortmunder* now widely refers to stronger lagers brewed for export, though not necessarily from Dortmund.

Among the best: Baltika 7 Export, Great Lakes Dortmunder Gold, Dab Original, Kona Longboard Lager

Eisbock

This is the strongest type of bock. It is made by chilling a doppelbock until ice is formed. At this point, the ice is removed, leaving behind a brew with a higher concentration of alcohol. This also serves to concentrate the flavors, and the resultant beer is rich and powerful, with a pronounced malt sweetness and a warm alcoholic finish. Alcohol levels start at about 9 percent ABV and go well into double digits.

Among the best: Eisbock 28, Schneider Avintinus Weizen-Eisbock, Kulmbacher Reichelbrau Eisbock

"Light" and Reduced-Calorie Lagers

These are the newer brews that are so popular in a figure-conscious society. Essentially these are pale lager-style beers with fewer calories. Like all other "diet products," the objective is to maintain flavor while minimizing calories. This achieved quite successfully by some brands, despite the implausibility of the proposition.

Among the best: Sam Adams Light, Yuengling Light

Maibock/Pale Bock

Maibocks are medium- to full-bodied lagers whose alcohol content approximates that of a traditional bock. The color of pale bocks can vary from light bronze to deep amber; they are characterized by a sweet malty palate and subtle hop character. As the name would suggest, this is a bock style that traditionally appears in May as a celebration of a new brewing season. In a Germanic brewer's portfolio, it should conventionally have a less assertive character than other bock offerings that emerge later in the year.

Among the best: Rogue Dead Guy Ale, Victory St. Boisterous, Stoudt's Blonde Double MaiBock

Munich Helles

Originating in Munich, this style of lager was developed as an answer to the popularity of Czech lagers. Pale to golden in color, these beers traditionally tend to be quite malt-accented with a subtle hop character. They are generally weightier than standard pale lagers though less substantial than Dortmunder export styles. Some of the finest examples still come from the brewing center of Munich and are relatively easy to find in major US markets.

Among the best: Weihenstephaner Original, Hofbräu Original, Spaten Premium Lager

Pale Lagers

Pale lagers are the standard international beer style as personified by products from Miller to Heineken. This style is the generic spin-off of the pilsner style. Pale lagers are generally light- to medium-bodied with a light to medium hop impression and a clean, crisp malt character. Quality, from a flavor point of view, is variable within this style, and many cheaper examples use a proportion of non-malt additives such as rice or corn to reduce the production costs. Alcohol content can vary, with the upper end of the range being preferable if you want to get a true lager mouthfeel.

Among the best: Stella Artois, Samuel Smith's Pure Brewed Lager Beer, Samuel Smith's Organically Produced Lager Beer

Pilsner

Pilsner styles of beer originate from Bohemia in the Czech Republic. They are medium- to medium-full-bodied and characterized by high carbonation and tangy Czech varieties of hops that impart floral aromas and a crisp, bitter finish. The hallmark of a fresh pilsner is the dense, white head. The alcohol levels should impart a rounded mouthfeel, typically around 5 percent ABV. Classic pilsners are thoroughly refreshing, but they are delicate and must be fresh to show their best. Few beers are as disappointing to the beer lover as a stale pilsner. German pilsner styles are similar, though often slightly lighter in body and color. Great pilsners are technically difficult to make and relatively expensive to produce.

Among the best: Czechvar, Pilsner Urquell, Victory Prima Pils

Rauchbier

The origins of rauchbier lie with breweries in the region of Franconia in northern Bavaria, which traditionally dried the barley over fires fueled by beech trees from local forests. The resulting pungent malt imparted an assertively smoky aroma and flavor to the beer made from it. These smoked lagers generally feature a very malty framework on which the intensely smoky character will not become overbearing. Rauchbiers are still brewed in the traditional manner by many of the breweries centered on the town of Bamberg, though enterprising brewers in other parts of the world have begun to make similarly styled beers.

Among the best: Rauch Ür Bock, Aecht Schlenkerla Rauchbier Märzen

Vienna-Style Lagers and Märzen/Fest Beers

The classic amber to red lager that was originally brewed in Austria in the nineteenth century has come to be known as the Vienna style. These are reddish amber with a very malty toasted character and a hint of sweetness. This style of beer was adapted by Munich brewers, and in their hands has a noted malty sweetness and toasted flavor with a touch more richness. The use of the term *märzen,* which is German for "March," implies that the beer was brewed in March and lagered for many months. On a label, the words *fest märzen* or *Oktoberfest* generally imply the Vienna style. Oktoberfest beers have become popular as September seasonal brews among US craft brewers, though they are not always classic examples of the German or Austrian style.

Among the best: Paulaner Oktoberfest Märzen, Hacker-Pschorr Original Oktoberfest, Spaten Oktoberfest Ur-Märzen, Victory Festbier

SPECIALTIES/HYBRIDS

Cream Ale

Cream ale is a North American specialty that is somewhat of a hybrid in style. Despite the name, many brewers use both ale and lager yeasts for fermentation and have been known to add a bit of lager beer. This style of beer is fermented like an ale at warm temperatures, but then stored at cold temperatures for a period of time, much as a lager would be. The resultant brew has the unchallenging crisp characteristics of a light pale lager, but is endowed with a hint of the aromatic complexities that ales provide. Pale in color, they are generally more heavily carbonated and more heavily hopped than light lagers.

Among the best: New Glarus Spotted Cow, Lagunitas Sirius Ale, Terrapin Golden Ale

Herb-Spiced and Fruit Beers

These are lagers or ales to which herbs, fruits, or spices have been added in order to impart flavor or color. Depending on whether or not the seasonings have been used in the fermentation or as an addition of juice or extract, the beer will have more or less of the desired character.

These beers are highly individualistic and allow brewers great creativity in their formulations. They range from mild aromatic overtones to intense and pungently flavored concoctions.

Among the best: Dogfish Head Midas Touch Golden Elixir, New Glarus Wisconsin Belgian Red, Magic Hat #9, Abita Purple Haze, Melbourn Bros. Strawberry

3

A PRIMER ON BEER
AND FOOD PAIRINGS

I've done quite a bit of freelance writing over the years, with much of my work appearing in culinary magazines. I find working for that sector to be enjoyable, as I like matching beer with what I'm going to eat. For the longest time, finding a good restaurant with a decent beer lineup was a problem. The situation seems to be getting a little better, but still exists. If you are anything like me, you know the deal. You're seated at a table and the first question asked of you is, "Would you like to see the wine list?" My standard reply is to ask for the beer list!

The wine menu is well designed, of course. Hey, if it's going to cost you $450 for that bottle of 1984 Opus One, it sure as hell better be printed on something that looks expensive.

Usually the beer "list" is handwritten on a sheet of notebook paper. Don't count on the server giving it to you; she'll read it to you instead.

In one of my more memorable visits to a classy dining establishment, the above scenario played out pretty much as described. My call to see the beer list was met with the comeback, "I'll see if we have one."

A few minutes later, she returned and said, "Our beers include Coors Light, Budweiser, Bud Light, and Heineken." After a period of silence, I asked, "Do you have any craft beers?" She answered, "Oh yes, we have Sam Adams!"

Now we're getting somewhere. Asking, "What flavors do you have?" got me the reply, "You mean they make more than one?"

Such is the dilemma. Why do so many fine dining restaurants maintain distinguished wine inventories at the expense of beer? I discussed just that with Canadian-born Marnie Old, certified an advanced sommelier by the Court of Master Sommeliers and director of wine studies at the French Culinary Institute in New York. In her words, "The responsibility to choose beer is often delegated to someone who 'likes it,' a senior bartender or chef. These people will frequently buy what they like rather than attempting to offer a range of styles. This creates those odd skewed selections where all beers are similar in style. To be perfectly frank, most restaurateurs have no interest in improving the beer selection, even if they like to drink it themselves. In fact, quite the opposite is true. There are serious downsides to building beer sales in fine dining, and most restaurants actively discourage them."

One of those downsides is the simple fact that beer is less expensive than wine. This equates to less customer spending, leading to the potential for a smaller stipend for the server.

Change occurs slowly, but there are signs of better days to come. In New York, there is at least one restaurant that employs a beer sommelier. I visited there and found approximately 110 beers available, many of which were from Belgium.

Perhaps the ultimate gathering for both beer aficionados and "foodies" took place in 2008 in Washington, DC, at an event called Savor: An American Craft Beer & Food Experience. A sellout crowd of twenty-one hundred people got to taste beers from forty-eight of the top craft breweries paired with assorted dishes. For example, you could try beers such as Allagash Black, Dogfish Head World Wide Stout, Flying Dog's Gonzo Imperial Porter, Rogue's Russian Imperial Stout, Santa Cruz Mountain Brewing's Devout Stout, and others paired with assorted flavors of Christopher Elbow Spiced Artisan Chocolates. Speakers at Savor included such luminaries as *The Wall Street Journal*'s Ken Wells, author of *Travels with Barley: A Journey Through Beer Culture in America;* Dave Lieberman from the Food Network; Ray Isle, senior wine editor at *Food & Wine* magazine; and assorted starts from the beer world, including Boston Beer's founder

Jim Koch, Dogfish Head founder Sam Calagione, and Brooklyn Brewing's brewmaster Garrett Oliver. What this event and others like it are doing is to legitimize the flavors of beer and demonstrate its flexibility as an accompaniment to a meal. Craft beer drinkers and some food lovers get it, but many still don't.

Perhaps part of the problem originates from the belief among the masses that beer doesn't pair as well with food as does wine. To their benefit, Marnie Old and Dogfish Head Brewery's Sam Calagione have hosted beer/wine dinners, in which patrons receive a matching beer and wine with each serving. I've participated in several such events, working with a wine expert. We sampled the menu roughly three weeks prior to the actual dinner, took notes, and gave the restaurant's general manager a listing of the beverages we recommended. Our dinner was structured in a light, jovial manner as the wine critic and I explained our logic for the pairings. After each serving, the audience completed a ballot and chose the beverage they felt was the best. Although wine won three of the five courses, the overall vote tally went to beer by a slight margin. Personally, I prefer working a wine-friendly house; it's kind of like playing on the road. After all, why preach to the choir?

When it comes to the marriage of beer and food, there is no one better than Garrett Oliver, author of *The Good Beer Book* (with Timothy Harper; Putnam/Berkley Books) and *The Brewmaster's Table: Discovering the Pleasures of Real Beer with Real Food* (HarperCollins). Over the last fifteen years, Oliver has appeared on most major television networks promoting beer's relationship with food. *The New York Times* presented a feature on him in which he is quoted as saying, "To me, beer and wine are both beverages meant to be served with food. And good beer, real beer, often offers things that most wine does not, like carbonation and caramelized and roasted flavors, aspects that sometimes make beer the preferable choice."

All that aside, let's start with a couple of assumptions. Generally speaking, light meals, in both substance and flavor, tend to match nicely with light beers. With reference to the brew, I lean to the less aggressive flavors with limited hop bitterness or bite. A generality to keep in mind is this: You can have flavors of food and beverage that complement or contrast. Here are two examples. A hot or spicy dish such as chorizo, which is a pork sausage that can be seasoned with chili or paprika, can benefit by being served with an India or American pale ale, both of which have an intense hop presence. It's almost like fighting fire with fire. That's an example of complementary flavors. Opting to go with something not quite as aggressive, like a lighter lager, might be a good way to douse that flame. That's what I mean by competing or opposite flavors coming into play. Fortunately, there are no hard-and-fast rules to worry about—like the old admonition of drinking white wines only with fish or fowl, a statement once thought of as sacred.

What follows below is a representative sampling of some food and beer unions. I cannot stress enough that you remain the final judge as to the viability of any coupling. You can read my recommendations, surf the Internet, or pick up other books or magazines that offer tips and gauge the advice given for yourself. Ultimately, you are the final critic, and that's how it should be.

After reading the information that follows, I'll describe three areas in which beer is enjoying success in the culinary world. One should not surprise you; the other two might (but an astute reader will catch on).

Lastly, certain styles of beer make for fine aperitifs. Hoppy beers such as pilsners and certain pale ales tend to stimulate the appetite. But do limit your guests and yourself to just one, as carbonation tends to cause a bloated feeling.

Apple Pie	Baltic Porter
	Sweet Stout
Bacon (Smoked)	Belgian Dubbel
	Alt
	Scottish Ale
	Rauchbier
Bass	Hefeweizen
	Wit
	Pilsner

Beef Carbonnade	Brown Ale
	Belgian Dubbel
Beef Wellington	Brown Ale
Beef Stew	Brown Ale
Boar	Brown Ale
	Doppelbock
	Scottish Ale
	Porter
Bouillabaisse	Belgian Tripel
	Saison
Buffalo	Brown Ale
	Porter
Buffalo wings	Pilsner
	Amber Ale
Burritos	American Pale Ale
	Rauchbier
	Brown Ale
Calamari (Fried)	Pilsner
	American Pale Ale
	Saison
Caviar	Pilsner
	Golden Ale
Cheese (Blue)	Dry Stout
	Barleywine
	Golden Ale
Cheese (Brie)	Sweet Stout
	Fruit Lambic
Cheese (Cottage, Cream)	Vienna Lager
	Amber Lager
	Hefeweizen
Cheese (Edam, Cheddar, Swiss)	Strong Ale
	Wit
	American Pale Ale
	India Pale Ale

Cheese (Feta)	Brown Ale
	Dry Stout
	India Pale Ale
Cheese (Mozzarella)	Hefeweizen
	Wit
	Weizen Bock
Cheese (Stilton)	Barleywine
	Strong Ale
Cheese (Trappist, Gouda, American)	Golden Ale
	Brown Ale
	Bock
Cheesecake	Fruit Lambic
	Belgian Dubbel
	Porter
	Sweet Stout
Chicken (Barbecued)	Brown Ale
	Golden Ale
	Amber Lager
	Porter
Chicken (Fried)	Amber Ale
	Amber Lager
	Brown Ale
Chicken (Roasted, Broiled)	Dark Lager
Chicken Cordon Bleu	Vienna Lager
Chili	American Pale Ale
	India Pale Ale
	Brown Ale
	Stout
Chocolate (Dark)	Fruit Lambic
	Sweet Stout
	Barleywine
Chocolate (Milk)	Fruit Lambic
	Fruit Beer
	Porter
	Dry Stout

Chocolate Cake	Sweet Stout
	Oatmeal Stout
	Imperial Stout
Clams	Pilsner
	Hefeweizen
Cod	Bitter
	Pilsner
	Amber Ale
Coffee	Barleywine
	Strong Ale
	Belgian Dubbel
Coq au Vin	Saison
	Belgian Dubbel
Corn on the Cob	Hefeweizen
Crab Cakes	Wit
	Golden Ale
	Blonde Ale
Duck	Belgian Dubbel
	Saison
Eggs (Scrambled)	Hefeweizen
	Wit
	Kristall Weizen
Fish-and-Chips	Bitter
	Pilsner
	Amber Ale
Fruit Salad	Hefeweizen
	Fruit Lambic
Goulash	Vienna Lager
	Pilsner
Green Salad (Cream Dressing)	Bock
Green Salad (Oil-Based, Vinaigrette Dressing)	Hefeweizen
	Wit
	Fruit Lambic
Haddock	Dunkel
	Hefeweizen
	Rauchbier

Ham (Baked)	Pilsner
	Belgian Tripel
	Maibock
Hamburger	Brown Ale
	Amber Ale
	Schwarzbier
Hummus	Hefeweizen
Ice Cream	Sweet Stout
	Porter
	Fruit Beer
Jambalaya	Vienna Lager
	India Pale Ale
	American Pale Ale
Kebabs	Brown Ale
	Irish Red
Lamb (Roasted)	Belgian Dubbel
	Scottish Ale
	Biere de Garde
	Strong Ale
Lasagna	Vienna Lager
	Amber Lager
	Amber Ale
Lemon Meringue Pie	Baltic Porter
	Fruit Beer
Lo Mein	Dunkel
	Hefeweizen
Lobster	Pilsner
	Stout
	Hefeweizen
	Wit
Macaroni and Cheese	Bitter
Meat Loaf	Brown Ale
Melons	Fruit Lambic
	Hefeweizen

Monkfish	Belgian Dubbel
	Bitter
	Brown Ale
	Hefeweizen
Mozzarella Sticks	Pilsner
	Amber Ale
	Belgian Dubbel
	Bock
Nachos	American Pale Ale
	India Pale Ale
Nuts	Brown Ale
	Belgian Dubbel
Osso Buco	Doppelbock
	Strong Ale
	Belgian Dubbel
Oysters	Sweet Stout
Pasta with Meat Sauce	Vienna Lager
	Pilsner
Pasta with Seafood	Hefeweizen
Pâté	Belgian Dubbel
	Brown Ale
	Strong Ale
Pizza	Vienna Lager
	American Pale Ale
Popcorn	Pilsner
	Hefeweizen
	Wit
Pork Tenderloin	Brown Ale
	Irish Ale
	Bock
Pretzels	Bock
Pumpkin Pie	Fruit Beer (Pumpkin)
	Herb-Spiced Beer

Quiche	Hefeweizen
	Wit
Ribs (Barbecued)	Vienna Lager
Risotto	Saison
	Belgian Tripel
Roast Beef	Porter
	Pale Ale (Various Styles)
Salami	Pilsner
	Saison
Salmon	Hefeweizen
	Wit
	Saison
	Pilsner
Salsa	American Pale Ale
	India Pale Ale
	Saison
	Pilsner
Sausage	Rauchbier
Shrimp	Hefeweizen
	Wit
	Pilsner
Snapper	Pilsner
	Saison
	Wit
Soup (Beef or Vegetable)	Brown Ale
	Porter
Soup (French Onion)	Scottish Ale
	Bock
Steak	Porter
	India Pale Ale
	Brown Ale
	Vienna Lager
Strawberries	Fruit Lambic
	Baltic Porter
	Imperial Stout

Sushi	Hefeweizen
	Wit
	Kristall Weizen
Trout (Smoked)	Rauchbier
Trout (Grilled, Broiled)	Kristall Weizen
	Alt
	Dunkel
	Hefeweizen
Tapas	Pilsner
Tiramisu	Fruit Lambic
	Fruit Beer
	Flavored Stout
	Oatmeal Stout
Tuna	Saison
	American Pale Ale
Turkey	Vienna Lager
Venison	Doppelbock
	Bock
	Scottish Ale
	Brown Ale

Have you figured out the three areas that are helping to accelerate the marriage of beer and food? The first should be easy, but the others probably are tougher. Here they are:

GRILLING

Grilling once was thought of as seasonal, especially in those areas that experience cold seasons. That no longer is the case. I was once of that mind-set, too. Grilling for many now is a twelve-month activity. We shovel a clearing to the grill out back or on the deck and cook in virtually any weather. No longer is the grill used only for meats; you also can cook fish and vegetables with confidence.

If you are having your friends visit for a cookout, you can bet the first two questions asked are "How do you want your meal cooked?" and "Would you like a beer?" Until the craft beer revolution took hold, we thought of only one type of beer for all foods, and that was the American lager. And frankly, you'd better have some of it on hand because of its thirst-quenching capacity, especially if you are outdoors on a warm day. Today, though, the connotation of barbecuing is broader than it was as recently as a decade ago, as people recognize that there are myriad flavors awaiting, some of which may be enhanced by the types of barbecue sauces or marinades used. It is this adaptability that makes beer, coming in a wealth of styles, the perfect drink to complete your meal.

When I think of barbecued foods, the three S's come to mind: spicy, smoky, and sweet. The types of beers that add to those impressions could include porters or stouts, rauchbiers, and pale ales. Please don't fall for the "I don't like dark beers because they're too heavy" syndrome. There is no relationship between a beer's color and its viscosity or alcohol content. Yet porters and stouts are hearty; bold enough to stand up to the robust flavors created from barbecuing beef.

Both porters and stouts are known for their roasted aromas, though I prefer to think of the latter as the "big brother" in the relationship because they tend to be a bit drier and more bitter. Guinness Draught surely comes to mind when thinking of a representative of this style. Either a porter or a stout should serve most beef dishes well.

Although a bit harder to find, smoked beers pair wonderfully with just about any barbecued food. Ranging in color from amber to dark brown, a classic rauchbier can be quite subtle or aggressive in smokiness. However, the better rauchbiers have a delicate harmony in their treatment of smoke, hops, and malt properties. Incidentally, there are some very good smoked porters available. Ask your packaged goods salesperson for help in choosing the right one.

The ale category is exhaustive. Some can be extremely bitter due to the type and amount of hops used; others are milder and somewhat sweet. Scottish ales, for example—amber to dark brown in color—

tend to be malty (somewhat sweet) but are offset by just enough hop bitterness to stop the beer from being too intense. There also may be a slight roasty, chocolatey, or even smoke-like quality.

Some brown ales are worthy of attention based upon their slightly nutty traits. You must take note of the type of beer under consideration as some browns, primarily American-style, are stronger and more bitter.

There are marked differences in the taste of barbecued pork and most beefs. Because pork is a bit sweeter, try to match it with a beer that is less hoppy (bitter) than you might choose for beef. In this instance, go for an amber ale, having a distinct caramel flavor, intended to balance the sharpness of the hops used.

As people become more accustomed to barbecuing and grilling different foods, the likelihood of finding an appropriate beer as an accompaniment grows in proportion.

Poultry is one of the most versatile foods for joining with beer. The key is in the preparation of the dish. The plainer the meal, the lighter the beer. Chicken marinated in a fruit/spice mix is made for a golden ale, generally with a subtle balance between sweet and bitter, although some brands can be on the fruity side. This is a style of beer that won't outdo the purity of the chicken.

Another noteworthy alternative is fruit beers. Practically any style of beer from stout to wheat to lager can exist in this variety, supplemented by the addition of the appropriate fruit in the brew. By joining a food marinated in a fruit base with a beer similarly fashioned, an excellent counterpart is produced.

If the dish is so hot you need to call 911 to put out the blaze, you have two options, which seem to be 180 degrees apart from one another. You can try to douse the flame by having a light-bodied beer such as a lager, or you can go for something highly hopped, like an American or Indian pale ale.

Just by the nature of the brewing process, lagers are known for their smoothness and crisp character. Think of beers such as Budweiser, Corona, and Pilsner Urquell as symbols of this grouping. Pale ales also furnish the much-needed rejuvenating effect, but the hop bitterness can stand up to the strong flavor and intricacy of the food. It's just a matter of personal choice.

When serving shellfish, or grilling tuna or salmon, the pure, tangy flavors of a wheat makes for a striking alliance. As with most beer styles, this family of drinks comes in varying forms, based in part on color. Furthermore, it is not uncommon for one class of this beer, hefeweizen, to appear cloudy because of the presence of suspended yeast particles. A high degree of carbonation is the norm. Wheats are known for their banana/clove aroma, which carries forward to the taste, ending with a remarkably light finish.

Another option is a similarly styled witbier, known for a citrus/spice smell and linked with the taste of orange and coriander. Witbiers also complement fish extraordinarily well. Wheat-based beers work well with vegetarian dishes, such as peppers, sweet corn, mushrooms, and squash.

Probably the last things you might expect to grill are fruits. As with vegetables, grilling an assortment of firm fruits at low to medium heat brings out amazing flavors as the natural sugars begin to caramelize. Let your imagination and the accessibility of fresh produce be your guide. Whichever you choose, you again will find a variety of fruit beers available both from the United States and from other countries, especially Belgium. Become familiar with the words *framboise* (raspberry), *kriek* (cherry), and *pêche* (peach) among the Belgian ales, for combinations that will send you to your epicurean utopia.

There aren't many drinks better suited to barbecuing and grilling than beer. Regardless of style, strength, and color, the flavors within a beer will enrich your food, and vice versa. Use some of the tips suggested but don't be afraid of experimentation. That's part of the charm of this superb beverage.

CHEESE

Think of a beverage to match with an assortment of cheeses and wine generally comes to mind. Part of the reason is perception. Let's face it, in most parts of the world wine is thought of as being more chic than beer. In reality, the notion of a wine and cheese union as a social event is a fairly recent concept, dating back only three or four decades. The teaming of beer with cheese, however, goes back to the Middle Ages, when Belgian monasteries became renowned for making both items, important parts of the everyday diet. The competition among abbeys to produce the finest cheeses was intense. It was during this time that many new types of cheeses came to being. Today many of the world's finest cheeses come from Denmark, France, Germany, Great Britain, Greece, Holland, Italy, Spain, Switzerland, and the United States.

It's not a stretch to recognize similarities in the production of both cheese and beer. Both are farmhouse products. It wasn't that many years ago that the typical British farmer's nutritional regime consisted of cheese (made on premises), bread, and a pint of beer, commonly referred to as a "ploughman's lunch." The cheese was made when there was an excess supply of milk. Brewing was done during the winter months when it was impractical to farm. And the origin of both is grass. Cows eat it, making a by-product called milk. Beer is based on a type of grass known as barley. Both result because of fermentation, with beer delivering alcohol and cheese forming acid. And of course, both practices have evolved over time.

Noted beverage writer Fred Eckhardt remarked, "Over the centuries, beer has become the sophisticated and wide-ranging delight that we know and love. In recent years, large companies may have reduced the brewing process to the lowest levels conceivable in their attempts to satisfy the most people possible. Despite that, modern beer is undergoing a revolution in which the old styles are being brought back and new styles are evolving. Beer is alive and moving right along. Cheese, too, has undergone a similar revolution. Cheese Whiz and Velveeta are no longer the epitome of mass-marketed cheese, and more than 'lite' beer is that of the beer industry. Small American cheese makers are undertaking the manufacture of ever more obscure cheese types from across the world, just as craft brewers have revived ancient and artisanal brewing processes."

Handcrafted cheeses are becoming much more readily available than they were even a decade ago. Although you may find some exceptional varieties in supermarkets, consider shopping at a reputable cheese purveyor who will allow you to sample the product prior to the sale. If possible, make your acquisition close to the time during which you'll be eating the cheese, in order to ensure maximum freshness. Keep in mind that the cheese you are sampling at the store probably has been refrigerated, and cold items tend to have a subdued flavor. After your purchase, wrap the cheese in aluminum foil or plastic wrap and chill it. This will keep the moisture in. Then remove it from the fridge and let it warm for about an hour or two prior to serving.

Another option is the Internet, which has some excellent cheese sources. There are a number of search engines that provide good references. Although I favor making my purchases from a reliable vendor, I have had success with online deals.

So how do you go about pairing cheese with beer, perhaps for a group of friends? Here are some tips:

- Assemble four to six cheeses for sampling. As an accompaniment, have mild crackers or bread available. Start with the more restrained cheeses, which generally will be put together with light (in taste) beers, then progress to the more aggressive, full-bodied combinations.
- Allow the cheeses to warm before serving. This will bring out the maximum flavor and aroma.
- For small get-togethers, permit your guests to cut directly from the cheese wedges or blocks.
- For larger groups, cut the cheese ahead of time, but incorporate a larger wedge on your serving plate to build an attractive presentation.
- Figure on about four ounces of cheese per person.
- Offer adjuncts appropriate to the cheese. Also include a selection of fresh or dried fruits and nuts.

The following combinations would make an ideal tasting sampler:

- *Mascarpone* is an Italian cheese that is solidified yet creamy. It's used as an ingredient in soups, pastas, and desserts. It can be spread onto crackers as a snack. Team it with a wheat beer or a Belgian-style saison and the sharp flavor of the beverage will contrast with the buttery richness of the cheese.
- *Brie* is probably the best-known French cheese. It is velvety and spreadable at room temperature. It frequently is served for dessert and supplements fruits, such as grapes or figs. A chocolatey stout or even a fruit lambic, traditionally brewed with wild yeasts and infused with fruit such as cherries, raspberries, or peaches, goes well.
- *Gorgonzola* and *blue cheeses* are known for their sharp flavors. You'll detect veins of blue or blue-green veins within. Blue can be soft or firm and crumbly. Both commonly are used in salads and dips. Match a more robust beer with either. A Trappist beer that is bottle-conditioned (yeast sediment at the bottom of the barrel) has a complex flavor profile that balances with the unique mold-ripened cheese taste.
- *Gouda* is a semi-soft to hard natural cheese, depending on its origin. It can be served as a table cheese or a dessert cheese. The flavor is light, sweet, and buttery. Smoked Gouda tends to be a bit firmer and nuttier. Serve it with a rauchbier (smoked beer) or a malty (sweet) bock beer. The former will complement the flavor while the latter will contrast.
- *Provolone* is a semi-hard, broad-spectrum cheese that tastes mild and buttery when young, although it can become sharp, smoky, or spicy as it ages. You'll see provolone used as a pizza topping or as a sandwich cheese. Selecting a beer can take you in a couple of directions. A lager will add a malty, biscuity profile that complements the young cheese, whereas the hop bitterness of a pale ale works nicely with aged provolone.
- *Parmigiano* and *Romano* are so hard, full seventy-five-pound wheels of them must be cut by a saw. Consequently, they are grating cheeses and are used in soups, pasta dishes, veal, chicken, or salads. The best Parmigiano is unpasteurized and is made from skimmed cow's milk. A portion of this combined with an India pale ale's hoppiness (bitterness) makes a superb alliance.

In some cases, a brewery is directly responsible for the flavor of the cheese, much in the manner of a few hundred years ago. Chimay Grande Reserve Trappist Ale and Chimay Trappist Cheese is such a union. This rich cheese actually is washed in the beer, creating flavors of fruit, nut, spices, and more.

Sample the cheese much the way you might taste a beer. Bring your senses into play. Look at the color and texture. Smell it. Then taste and evaluate.

The subject of the cheese's rind, if there is one, generally concerns whether it is edible. Actually, there are many variations. Fresh cheese has no rind. These often are tub cheeses, such as cottage cheese.

A "natural" rind occurs when the outer edges harden spontaneously from contact with the air. This grouping includes the blue cheeses. Some hard cheeses such as cheddar and Parmigiano Reggiano have natural rinds. The formation of some natural rinds is augmented by a non-invasive procedure that causes a layer of mold to grow on the exterior of the rind. This prevents air from getting in and furthering internal mold. Bloomy or surface mold rinds have a growth of mold as a result of a spraying of a mold spore solution. Cheeses such as Brie and Camembert employ this method. The mold then is cleaned off after a few days, leaving a dark, hard protection that may or may not be eaten. A washed rind comes about when the cheese is bathed in water, brine, beer, wine, or a combination, in order to encourage a bacterial growth. The color will range anywhere from yellow to red. You'll also remember the smell; they are very stinky! Consequently, these rinds seldom are eaten.

Some cheeses receive a coating of ash, wax, or other materials, also serving as a shielding agent.

Feel free to experiment with beer and cheese combinations. You'll find that, given the right setting, the malt/hop profile of the drink will harmonize with the smooth consistency and mouthfeel of cheese. Unlike any other beverage, beer has the ability to elevate those flavors to their fullest.

Cheese Facts
• More cheese is consumed during the end-of-year holidays in America than any other time of the year.

- The best-selling cheese in the United States is cheddar, followed by mozzarella.
- Wisconsin produces more cheese than any other state.
- Americans consume about thirty pounds of cheese per person annually. The world leaders are the French and Greeks, who eat about fifty pounds per person.
- Swiss cheese gets its holes because of the development of carbon dioxide during the time in which the cheese is ripening.
- There are over three hundred different varieties of American-made cheese.
- About a third of the milk produced annually in the United States goes to make cheese.
- Hard cheeses generally store for longer periods of time than softer ones because the hard cheeses have lower moisture.
- Cheese can be frozen, but it may become crumbly after thawing. Flaky cheese can be used in salads or as toppings.
- Cheeses such as Swiss and cheddar contain virtually no milk sugar (lactose). Most of it is removed during production.

GOUDA CHEESE AND BEER SPREAD
Prep time: 15 minutes
Makes 16 servings

4 ounces cream cheese
⅓ cup sliced green onions
1½ tablespoons spicy brown mustard
8 ounces shredded regular or smoked Gouda cheese
⅓ cup beer, preferably a lager
Paprika
Cocktail rye bread, rye crisps, or crackers
Fresh-chopped chives

Place the cream cheese, green onions, and mustard in a food processor. Process until combined. Add the shredded Gouda cheese and beer; process until well blended. Transfer to a bowl and sprinkle paprika on top of spread. Cover and chill at least 2 hours or up to 24 hours before serving with rye bread, rye crisps, or crackers. Garnish with chopped fresh chives.

Beer pairing: Rauchbier (smoked beer) if the cheese is smoky; otherwise, go with a bock beer (a type of lager).

DESSERT

If you read the chart carefully, you saw a few food items normally served after the main course. Matching desserts with beer is trendy and showcases the suppleness of several styles of the beverage. There now are restaurants offering beer-and-dessert specials, especially during evening hours of operation.

Think of it . . . you've just completed a hearty meal and are settling in for dessert. Looks like cherry cheesecake is going to be served. And the accompanying beverage? Sure, coffee may be fine, but a porter or stout matches perfectly!

Keep all the principles with other servings in mind. Neither the food nor the beer should be so strong as to dominate the other.

Stouts or porters are united by their dark color (think of Guinness, for example). Porters tend to be sweeter than stouts as the flavor is driven more by the malts used, rather than from roasted grain. Actually, porters predated stouts. Known in England and colonial America as the drink of the "commoner," legend has it that when the alcohol content of porter was increased, the name *stout porter* emerged, eventually becoming simply stout.

Although chocolate desserts team up marvelously with both types of beer, there are subdivisions of each style that could influence your preferences. Of course, that becomes a matter of choice.

One of the best stouts you'll find is Young's Luxury Double Chocolate Stout, from the Ram Brewery in England. Young's uses real dark chocolate and chocolate essence in the recipe. In fact, melted chocolate bars are added to the boil. By the way, Ram Brewery is the oldest site in Britain at which beer has been brewed continuously.

Brooklyn Brewery's Black Chocolate Stout is based on a variety known as Russian Imperial Stout, made by British brewers for the Russian Imperial Court in the nineteenth century. Brooklyn's adaptation is a bit sweeter than I prefer as a stand-alone, but serving it with a dark chocolate cake is perfection. Personally, I fancy a scoop of vanilla ice cream placed in a pint of Black Chocolate Stout, making the definitive shake!

Among porters, Sierra Nevada's contribution is superb. You may notice a coffee-like aroma, in concert with a chocolate malt taste.

Anchor Porter is similar to Sierra Nevada, although I detect a slight fruitiness in the former. Either drink is assertive enough to stand up to chocolate-based dishes, from mousse to cakes to puddings, and may be favored by those who don't like the intensity of stouts.

Because experimentation in food/beer pairings is encouraged, consider Belgian and Belgian-style ales for another option. Dubbels are dark in color and have a malty sweetness, fruity taste, and roasted nut aroma. Westmalle Dubbel is a remarkable case in point, with a malt aroma followed by chocolate and tropical impressions. Throw a bit of fresh fruit mix into the equation and you get the complete picture. Try this beer with a light chocolate, most fruits, or even cheesecake.

Originating in the Flanders region of Belgium, lambics are wheat beers that have been spontaneously fermented. In layman's terms, this refers to a procedure by which airborne yeasts that have been native to the area for hundreds of years are used to create what many feel are the most complex beers in the world.

After fermentation, the beer is relocated to casks where it develops for close to a year. Next, the lambic is moved to bottles, where it is joined with carbon dioxide and then sealed. About a year later, the liquid is ready for consumption.

There are further iterations of lambic. A gueuze is made when lambics of varying ages are blended, then refermented, for at least a year. The popular fruit lambics are made by combining the brew with fresh fruit before bottling. The most popular examples include raspberries (*framboise*), cherries (*kriek*), and peaches (*pêche*). The introduction of fruit sets off yet another round of fermentation, creating an intense effervescence that gives the finished product a champagne-like quality.

The most popular lambics are those made by Lindemans, Boon, Liefmans, Cantillon, Van Steenberge, and Hanssens. Be aware that not all lambics are identical in taste. Some may be sweeter or more tart.

Known as "the beer for those who claim they don't like beer," a fruit lambic can be drizzled over a portion of sorbet. Strawberry lambic makes a fine accompaniment to strawberry shortcake. Or how about a peach cobbler served with a fluted glass of *pêche*?

Below are two of my favorite combinations. As you can see, both are quite easy to make.

BEER FLOAT

1 bottle of your favorite porter or stout
1 scoop vanilla ice cream

Fill a soda glass with beer and add a scoop of vanilla ice cream. Garnish with a cherry.

SPECIAL SORBET

1 scoop fruit sorbet (peach, raspberry, cherry)
2 tablespoons fruit lambic, matching the flavor of the sorbet

Place a scoop of sorbet in an ice cream cup. Drizzle the lambic over the sorbet. Keep a glass of the remaining beer nearby for refreshment.

4

HOW DO I . . . ?:
BEER Q&As

I recall having dinner not too terribly long ago when the conversation among the people at a table next to me turned to beer. There were probably a dozen people there, and the selection of beverages was varied. "Beer is the new wine" was what a gentleman nearby said to the others. Hearing that, I attempted to eavesdrop. "There are so many good beers on the market today, and they match great with food," he added. I think I sent over a beer to him.

What that diner proudly stated seems to be a thought that is spreading around the country. We're behind much of the remainder of the world, however, in recognizing the flexibility of beer. Of course, we can't really be blamed heavily, considering the fact that the revolution in the beer world still is relatively new. Go back to the mid-1970s and there were only a few dozen American breweries, mostly making the same types of beer. Variety was nonexistent. Today there are close to fifteen hundred breweries of all sizes, although you'd have to undertake a major road trip to taste them all. Many are brewpubs and very small microbreweries that don't distribute too far from their doors.

. . . FIND THAT SPECIAL BEER?

So many times I hear people say that they've looked all over for a distinctive beer, possibly one that they really enjoyed at some time in the past. Finding that beer can be as complex as finding Osama bin Laden, but there are steps you can take to narrow the search. I highly recommend establishing a good relationship with one or two purveyors of beer. Get to know the key people there on a first-name basis. Let them see you when you are in the store so they'll know you are a valued customer.

Let's say that the Acme Brewing Company makes a killer brown ale, one that you loved. You want to find it and savor more of those moments. You've gone to your vendor and he carries a line of Acme beers, but you just don't see that brown ale. Assuming it was not a onetime brew, you should seek your contact at the store and ask for the desired flavor. Yes, he may be out of it at the time, but there could be a shipment due in shortly. Knowing you are a loyal regular customer will make it even more likely that he'll attempt to get your beverage for you. He may even call or email you when it arrives. If you have a second or even third retailer, check there as well.

Use the Internet to research your beer. Practically all breweries maintain websites. If your special beer isn't currently shipped to your locale but enough people demand it, you can bet every effort will be made to move into your region.

Be aware that a beer you may have relished in another part of the country may not be sold where you live. That's the nature of the business. Distribution costs being what they are, many small breweries service constituents in their immediate area first.

You have to be prepared for the possibility that you just won't be able to secure that unique beer despite your best efforts. Before giving up, exhaust all avenues.

. . . DECIDE WHAT BEER TO ORDER AT A BREWPUB?

Of the American companies that make beer, most fall into the category of brewpubs—places that make beer for on-site consumption. Attached restaurants are the rule, with food often rivaling that of the finest restaurants. For some time, the number of brewpubs in this country has hovered around the one thousand mark, although as with any business that can change week by week.

The number of beers served at any brewpub can vary, but I've seldom seen fewer than half a dozen on tap. Usually there are more. You walk into a brewpub and see those handles as the bartender asks, "What'll it be?" You'll probably pause for a while as you look over the beer list, either printed or displayed on a wall. Since this place may be new to you (or even if it's one you occasionally visit), your best bet is to ask for the "sampler." Hey, doing so will let your server know you are familiar with brewpubs, putting you one step ahead of almost everyone else. More important, you'll get a few ounces of everything being poured on that particular day!

What you'll commonly find is a light or low-alcohol beer. Be aware that this ain't your normal reduced-alcohol beer; it has a lot more flavor. As for the rest of their array, colors will vary; you'll see straw-colored beers and brown or almost brown ones. The key is in the presentation.

The serving area at La Birreria, a brewpub situated on the rooftop of Eataly, the gourmet food market in Manhattan. The area features a rotating array of regional beers.

If your server is educated in beer, he'll present the drinks to you lined up in a specific order. I've seen this occur in three manners, with one being totally unacceptable.

My preferred arrangement is receiving beers from least to most bitter or hoppy. The degree of bitterness goes a long way in affecting your interpretation of that which follows. Tasting a hoppy beer first can adulterate the next one, unless a fairly significant amount of time passes. You have eight beers in front of you; do you want to wait fifteen minutes between sips? I sometimes ask for a glass of water to accompany my beer because I want to take a short break between drinks. You'll observe that there is no pattern to the color, although I do suspect that a very softly shaded golden beer might be the first on the list. Also, whether a beer is clear or unfiltered is not a consideration.

You may be getting your beers from what is described as the least to most assertive in terms of flavor profile, normally as defined by the brewer. Once more, bet on the brewer's lightest in alcohol probably being the leadoff hitter, although an unfiltered beer, probably having a number of emerging flavors, could be near the end of your tasting cycle. Your dark, roasted flavors, such as stouts or porters, will fall near the end. Depending on the time of year, look for a seasonal to make the mix; where is appears is subject to the style.

You probably can guess a serving array that plainly is improper: the one in which beers are handed out according to color. Unfortunately, I've been witness to this setup. When this is the case, I question the degree to which the barkeep has been schooled in his products or whether the brewer or director of operations has a handle on what is going on. All this does is propagate the false belief that the most intense flavors come from the darkest of beers.

The beauty of purchasing a sampler comes from the fact that you almost certainly will find at least one or two flavors that you enjoy enough to order a pint. If you are planning on eating at the brewpub, your beer choice could influence what you will order. Also, there's a good chance you'll find recommended food and drink pairings on the menu.

Allow me to take a step onto the soapbox for a brief while. I've popped into brewpubs that have "guest" beers on tap. By that, I am referring to beers from other breweries, generally those from the giants of the industry. I once saw one establishment that framed out one tap handle, then two, finally three of its eight taps, leading me to question the owner's commitment to his beers and to wonder about the direction of the business.

Should you find a thoroughly enjoyable beer at the brewpub, you will have the opportunity to purchase a glass "growler" to take home. Poured right from the tap, a growler contains half a gallon of the beer, normally enclosed by a twist-off cap. It kind of looks like what you might expect a moonshiner to put his squeezin's in. The cost will vary

Many times the brewpub will provide several numbers to describe the beers being served. OG means "Original Gravity," a reading taken prior to fermentation. FG, "Final Gravity," is done after fermentation and defines how completely the yeast ferments available sugar. IBU is "International Bittering Units," a rough indicator as to how bitter a beer may be, depending upon style. Given two identical beers, the one with a higher IBU will be more bitter. ABV is "Alcohol By Volume."

from brewpub to brewpub, even based to a degree on the style of the beer, but expect to pay somewhere around ten dollars. After you drink the contents and return to the brewpub, you usually can have it refilled at a reduced price.

Don't expect the beer in a growler to remain fresh for very long. Bring it home and refrigerate it immediately and it can remain unopened for a week or maybe two, if you are lucky. Once opened, invite friends and family to partake with you because whatever is left over will turn overnight.

... SET UP A BEER TASTING IN MY HOME?

As with wines, people are setting up formal and informal home beer samplings, creating opportunities for aficionados as well as those simply interested in alternative flavors to explore the world of beer. I've been present both as a presenter and as a guest, and I can tell you the number of people in attendance has no limit, but is dependent upon the host and his level of comfort. Food generally is provided, ranging from a full-course dinner to hors d'oeuvres. Regardless, home tastings are fantastic social and learning events, especially when planned right. One thing you don't want is to leave your guests wanting more or not being able to sample effectively.

Certainly there are no rules for an occasion such as this, so the following is one of many ways to go about your event:

• *Use a season or holiday as your reference.* The types of beers you offer will be dependent on time of year. For example, in the fall you could go for Oktoberfest beers and present those that are available at that great celebration held annually in Munich. Blending an American version or two of an Oktoberfest beer can help you get a handle on how that brewer interpreted the style. During the warm-weather months, go with wheats. They are wonderful thirst quenchers and are perfect around a patio or pool.

- *Spotlight a brewery.* Many breweries, even the small ones, make more than one flavor. Having them for your home event is a good way to highlight most, if not all, of a company's portfolio. If you are able to contact the brewery or its distributor directly, there's a good chance you'll get some freebies, such as T-shirts, bottle openers, and such. Breweries are no different from any other corporations: They want your business.

- *Showcase a style.* In the first example, Oktoberfest beers are of one style, so this should be self-explanatory. I've seen some American pale ale events that pit beers of the East Coast versus those of the West Coast. The West Coast has a reputation for making some of the best APAs around, and some easterners take exception to that claim. Pick up a few of each and watch those hoppy, bitter beers make your mouth pucker from the high degree of citrus. Belgian ale tastings have been hugely popular for years and seem to attract interest among guests. This type of tasting is sometimes known as a horizontal tasting.

- *Set up an* Iron Chef *competition.* In a mild-mannered takeoff on the popular television series, some tastings offer an imported beer style—say, a Czech pilsner—paired with an American adaptation of the same. The new breed of American brewers have recognized the work of brewers from around the world and have placed their own mark on their creations. Are they better than the originals? Have your audience vote and see who wins. If you really want to have fun, do this as a blind tasting, meaning the beers aren't disclosed until after the pairs have seen sampled.

- *Host a vertical tasting.* A horizontal tasting deals with beers of a similar style; a vertical tasting showcases the same beer from different years. Obviously, if a vertical tasting is what you want, begin by aging your beers now. Be sure to read the next part of this chapter dealing with vintage beers.

In setting up your beer tasting, I'd recommend a minimum of five beers. Create a short listing of the beers you'll be serving, in the order of presentation. This doesn't have to be anything spectacular, but should allow your guests some room to record their thoughts on what was just sampled.

Be sure to have your beers chilled by the time your visitors arrive. Controlling the temperature will be difficult because, after all, you are the host, but try to keep your lighter beers (lagers, wheats) the coldest, most ales a bit warmer; go warmer still for the strongest of beers. You can control this to a extent by removing your bottles from the refrigerator at different times. Have a pitcher of water handy for use between beverages.

Certain types of beer flourish in the proper glassware, though you aren't running a bar. At the very minimum, select clear glasses. Many people go for clear plastics in a pinch. Under optimum conditions, a separate glass would be used for each beer. Realistically, that calls for far more glasses than you probably own, so weigh your options. Come cleanup time, you may feel plastics are a better choice.

For many, aesthetics play a role in beer appreciation. A good-looking beer just tastes better when served in its proper glassware. However, there seem to be as many types of receptacles as there are beers. And who wants to go out and buy a few hundred glasses?

A European tradition is to show the brewery's logo on their glassware. The concept has spread to our shores, where an increasing number of breweries have created drinking vessels that are meant to be paired with their products.

If having the right container is important to you, here is how to proceed. Concentrate your efforts on a few basic styles, which should safely see you through most beers. They are:

• *Pilsner.* You've seen them a million times. The shape is that of an inverted cone and is perfect for those aromatic hoppy ales. Pilsner glasses promote good head retention and uniform dispersal of carbonation.
• *Weiss tumbler.* Because weiss or wheat beers produce a large amount of foam, the weiss (or weizen) tumbler intensifies the yeasty, fruity aromas associated with this kind of beer.

- *Tulip.* These are perfect for fragrant beers, such as Belgian ales. A flared tulip is designed to allow the beer to move under the creamy layer of foam and into the mouth, while retaining the aromatics. A brandy snifter generally makes an acceptable substitute.
- *Goblet.* When the aroma of the beer is a bit more subdued than in the previous example, the goblet is perfect. Its shape encourages the beer's fragrance to come forward and the stem can be held to slightly warm the beverage.
- *Pint.* This is the most basic of all glasses and is the one most often found in bars, restaurants, and brewpubs. This is a slight swelling near the rim, which aids in handling and for promoting the distinctive aroma of hops. Pint glasses also are ideal for the roasted notes of stouts and porters.
- *Flute.* When serving fruit beers such as raspberry (*framboise*), cherry (*kriek*), or peach (*pêche*), a fluted glass centralizes and intensifies the bubbles and aroma, directing them to your nose.

Of equal importance is the cleanliness of the glass. Although there is no consensus of opinion as to how serving vessels should be washed and dried, be aware that any dishwasher residue left behind will dramatically affect head retention and will impart adverse flavors to the drink. Any lint or dust should be removed from the glass for similar reasons.

Refrain from chilling your glassware in the freezer prior to use. Frozen glasses will introduce ice into the beer, reducing the fullness of flavor. Extremely cold beer tends to lack the deep, rich flavors that come to the front when the beverage is served slightly warmer.

As for the amount of beer to be poured, stay in the three-ounce range, but have a bit left over for those who might want a refill. A twelve-ounce bottle supplies enough for four people and a large wine bottle, a 750ml size, can take care of about eight. The gray area arises if the beer is bottle-conditioned, having a bit of yeast sediment at the bottom. If the yeast cannot be mixed by gently swirling the bottle prior to pouring, consider, for this type of function, not dispensing the last few ounces. Keep that in mind as you make your purchase.

Keep conversation to a minimum but do welcome any comments from your guests. Some will just want to enjoy the beer without talk; others may offer comments. Candidly, after the first couple of beers, the odds of anyone remaining quiet are nil, so just roll with it.

. . . SELECT BEERS FOR AGING?

This may be the hottest topic going on in the beer world. The immense popularity of craft and imported beers has led to a spin-off effect, the placing of selected styles into storage for an extended time, not the normal shelf life of up to six months for most beers. In the words of a famous former president whose name escapes me, let me make one thing perfectly clear: Almost all beers should be consumed when they are as fresh as possible. Given that statement, there are certain styles, regardless of brand or origin, that can be cellared for years. By and large, your best candidates will have a high alcohol content and be bottle-conditioned, but that's not a rule that's written in stone. Shortly, I'll identify specific beers that will mature gracefully.

I have a few bottles of Christmas Ale by Anchor Brewing going back to 1982. I was given a few bottles from that year and each year until 2004. Since then, I've been adding bottles of each year's version (we could borrow the term *vintage* from the wine folks) to my domain and occasionally open one to share with friends or family.

If you're contemplating aging or "cellaring" beers, there are factors to take into consideration. It is paramount that you keep the bottles away from light as much as possible and in a constant cool environment. Many individuals take the word *cellar* literally and use that space as it exists. Truthfully, an area of my basement is reserved for that purpose along with a refrigerator dedicated to those beers that I probably will be drinking in the near future.

How a bottle is sealed can affect its longevity. If your bottle is capped, you shouldn't run into problems. More and more bottles now are corked, especially those of the 750ml variety. The question pertaining to whether they should be stored upright or on their side surfaces.

One thing I am not advocating is spending a ton of money to purchase a cabinet with humidor for storage purposes. I've seen wine cabinets that have cost over ten thousand dollars, but these are used to store individual bottles of wine that could fetch much more than any beer you or I might acquire. If I scored a bottle of Mouton Rothschild 1945, I'd want optimum conditions, too. In late 2006, a magnum of it sold for just under thirty thousand dollars!

Let's keep it real. If you are lucky enough to have storage space, it could be a cellar, an extra fridge, or possibly a spare cabinet. Regardless, your priorities should be coolness (no temperature variations) and darkness.

Still interested in vintage beers but don't have an aging room? There are options. A growing number of distributors are doing the work for you. One that I particularly favor is B. United International, an importer of wines, meads, ciders, sakes, beers, and more. In the late 1990s, they established a vintage beer division by cellaring hundreds of cases of selected beers from many of the beer-producing countries around the world. B. United's president, Matthias Neidhart, said, "In composing our collection, we had to draw from the experience of the great wineries of the world in cellaring their brands, as most breweries have no knowledge whatsoever about it. We had to create space to cellar hundreds and hundreds of cases in a temperature and light controlled environment. We intend to eventually have between 2,000 and 3,000 cases of different vintage items in our collection. We are working with our wholesalers to ensure that they arrive to you in the finest condition."

I've seen a few labels going back as far as twelve years. By going to their website (www.bunitedint.com) and clicking on the Vintage Collection link, you see the current inventory. In choosing a specific beer, you'll get tasting notes from industry experts, product details that include alcohol by volume, vintages, and bottle size. You also can find details about the brewery and occasionally suggested food pairings.

Growing legions of breweries now are utilizing some of their space to reserve a medley of their beers for sale as people visit for a tour. The Allagash Brewing Company, based in Portland, Maine, is known for their remarkable Belgian-style ales, but they've also retailed anniversary ales, already aged for at least a year. I've visited other breweries that do the same.

Advice on the longevity of a beer can come from a brewery itself. One such company that takes pride in the life of its beers is Unibroue, located in Quebec, Canada. Started in the early 1990s, Unibroue gained a reputation for making some of the most authentic Belgian-style beers outside Belgium. Interestingly, the current brewmaster, Paul Arnott, formerly served in that capacity at that country's world-famous Chimay brewery. Perhaps that explains his expertise. I once interviewed Paul and asked him point-blank why he left Chimay to go to Unibroue. He responded by asking me a question: "Gary, when was the last time you saw a new beer coming from Chimay?" Of course, I had no clue. He said, "Exactly. But at Unibroue I can release at least one new beer each year." A great comeback, and it helped explain the creativity in this man.

Here is what the company says about their beers:

- Blanche de Chambly is a partially filtered white (wheat) ale with a shelf life of eighteen months.
- Maudite is a mahogany-colored strong red ale with a hint of spice and citrus. The shelf life is at least five years.
- La Fin du Monde is golden in color with a 9 percent ABV level. There's fruit, spice, exceptional carbonation, and good balance between malt and hops. Expect this beer to last for three years.
- Trois Pistoles is a very dark ale that is not unlike a fine port. This beer will last for three years.
- Don de Dieu is a spiced wheat beer that should be fine for up to three years.

There are more in the company's portfolio, but I think you get the picture.

Now there are restaurants creating aged beer lists. One of the best is The Brickskeller in Washington, DC. The last time I was there, over fifty vintage beers were available for purchase.

During my one visit to Max's on Broadway in Baltimore, Maryland, an aged beer cooler made for a pleasant addition to what was an outstanding collection of tap beers.

One of the most influential people in the restaurant business is Danny Meyer, co-owner of New York City's Gramercy Tavern. I've dined at a few of his properties, all of which have decent beer menus, during my most recent stop at Gramercy I noticed over twenty different vintage beers on the menu and a few ciders. One of those beers was England's Thomas Hardy, dating back to 1993.

Forward-thinking merchants are getting into the act by establishing aging rooms for some of their brews. In Mount Holly, New Jersey, there is a small but very hip store called Red, White and Brew, known for selling beverages from small companies. Try finding a Budweiser in the place; it won't happen. The move toward selling only craft and imported beers was an of to what is going on at restaurants in the downtown district. One of the most popular establishments there, the High Street Grill, expanded the number of tap handles and removed all mass-marketed beers. Why? Those beers just weren't selling that well. Patrons would dine at the restaurant, sip a microbrew, and want to buy a six-pack of it across the street at the liquor store. Thus, management made the decision to only sell this type of product.

At Red, White and Brew, a small corner of the store was reserved for aged beers and proved to be popular. When I visited there a year or two after this was established, the vintage beer assortment had been expanded and moved into a cold room. As the word is getting out about how certain beers can age gracefully, sales are increasing.

In terms of what to expect from a cellaring program, I've found that any hoppy bitterness tends to mellow out in time. Much of the aroma will be lost. And if you're paying a visit to a restaurant or pub serving these beers, be prepared to pay a handsome price for a bottle. One twelve-ouncer easily can cost up to twenty dollars or more. I found a 750ml bottle of Interlude (2007) from Allagash that was selling for forty-four dollars. These ain't your daddy's prices.

Let's define those styles of beer that will provide the best chances for delicate aging. Do remember that multiple bottles of the same flavor do not ensure identical flavors over time. There just are too many outside stimuli that can alter what's going on within the bottle. The listing below is a representative sample of things that I've aged or have sampled. Feel free to experiment on your own.

Barleywines

Sierra Nevada Bigfoot Barleywine
Anchor Old Foghorn
Brooklyn Monster Ale
Avery Hog Heaven
Rogue Old Crustacean
Victory Old Horizontal

Porters and Stouts

Brooklyn Black Chocolate Stout
Dogfish Head World Wide Stout
Stone Imperial Russian Stout
Sinebrychoff Porter

Belgian and Belgian-Style

Chimay (Red, Blue)
Orval
Westmalle (Dubbel, Tripel)
Samiclaus
Victory Golden Monkey
Allagash Grand Cru
Ommegang (Three Philosophers, Hennepin)

Ommegang introduced a somewhat unusual, yet effective means of releasing their aged beers: placing hundreds of cases of their Hennepin, Three Philosophers, and Abbey Ale for storage in Howe Caverns, situated in the central part of New York State. Some people describe

Brewery Ommegang, based in Cooperstown, NY, is the maker of several award-winning Belgian-inspired ales, including Ommegang, Hennepin, Witte, Rare Vos and Three Philosophers.

this as an effective advertising ploy, but if you think of it, the practice of storing beer during summer months, for example, dates back hundreds of years. And how does this benefit Ommegang? The caves at Howe Caverns extend 156 feet below ground and the temperature remains at fifty-two degrees year-round. So what could be better for storing beer than this dark, cool, undisturbed environment?

Again, do not think of this as the definitive listing of beers that age well. It's only a beginning and represents those beers I've had that were from previous years.

What is there about high levels of alcohol that seem to prevent some beers from developing bad traits? One thing we know for sure is that the presence of ethyl alcohol is effective in retarding the development of those microorganisms that cause a beer to spoil. The more alcohol present, the longer it takes for a beer to turn bad. As a beer ages, alcohol reacts with other compounds that are present to yield fruity, wine-like aromas and flavors. Many vintage beers tend to have components of banana, apple, grape, and orange, for example—qualities that aren't objectionable. This change just doesn't occur in those beers with little alcohol.

Bottle-conditioned, unfiltered beers with a low amount of alcohol will not age as well as those with higher levels. Those are the beers with active yeast added at bottling time, the same yeast used during fermentation. As for why this type of beer can be more effectively stored than those that aren't bottle-conditioned, remember what the yeast still in the bottle does. Any remaining sugars are converted into alcohol and bubbles of carbon dioxide. Knowing that oxygen is an element that destroys a beer's essence and there is a tiny bit of oxygen in the bottle, the yeast more or less binds that oxygen, reducing instances of bad flavor.

Of course, the yeast does not stay alive forever. After about a year, the dead and decaying cells (sounds appetizing, huh?) can affect the flavor of the beer. This change could be positive or negative, depending on the strain of the organism and the style of beer. For this reason, some brewers filter their beer then add fresh yeast as a way to control future flavor.

You need to be aware of the fact that yeast cells are vulnerable to temperature variations. Warmth will speed the refermentation process and hasten the deterioration of those cells. Refrigeration will slow things down and add time to your aging beer, but will not stop what naturally is going to occur.

By now some of you may be wondering about the bitter, hoppy beers, such as the India pale ales (IPA). What a curious history to this style of beer, dating back to eighteenth-century England. Briefly, because back then the beer didn't survive the journey to the British troops stationed in warm climates without spoiling, extra hops and grain were added to existing pale ale, then shipped. The result was a highly bittered drink, very high in alcohol. The preservative effects of both the alcohol and hops ensured against contamination.

I've tried aging a few well-hopped beers, including Dogfish Head's 90 Minute IPA and Sierra Nevada Pale Ale, arguably two of the best of its type. What I experienced with that beer has been replicated with other India and American pale ales.

The smell of hops is influenced by the variety of hops used and when these are added. If included near the end of the boil, a fragrant floral or citrusy smell will emerge. What happens with these beers is a loss of that bouquet. Furthermore, bitterness tends to dwindle as the alpha acids responsible for flavor break down. Consequently, the beer you laid down will bear little resemblance, at least in flavor, to the original. The 90 Minute IPA comes in at 9 percent ABV, but the company brews a limited-edition bigger brother called 120 Minute IPA, weighing in at (gulp) 20 percent ABV. I've heard of individuals laying this down with a good deal of success.

You especially observant readers will note that there's been no mention of lagers, possibly a surprising omission given the fact that a lagered beer has already been aged for some time. Evidence suggests that the manner in which lagers are brewed in conjunction with a warm storage temperature leads to loss of flavor. I did age one lager, Paulaner Oktoberfest, for a year in a refrigerated environment and found degradation to be noticeable, but not to the point of being undrinkable. I then placed some of the bottles in my normal cellar conditions and witnessed a marked decline in quality within a matter of a few weeks. In this example, the cold definitely slowed down the harm to the beverage.

If you're selecting low-alcohol beers or possibly lagers for storage, consider opening up your bottles intermittently to check on flavor. If you see signs that the beer is on the verge of becoming unpleasant, then you can take the necessary corrections or just discard the product. Bear in mind that a beer that is turning will not do so overnight and some of those changes, although undesired, may still make for a reasonably acceptable beer.

At the beginning of this section, I mentioned that I have several bottles of Christmas Ale by Anchor Brewing going back to 1982. I wish I could take the credit for being so resourceful in obtaining and aging them, but I can't. Sports buffs will recognize the name Andy Musser, longtime voice of the Philadelphia Phillies baseball team. In his travels,

Andy, a beer aficionado, was able to visit some of the best breweries and pubs throughout the country. He met Fritz Maytag, owner of San Francisco's Anchor Brewing, and they immediately became friends based on Andy's love of his beverages and Fritz's enjoyment of the sport. Eventually, Andy began working for Anchor and, to this day, hosts speaking engagements and beer festivals where Maytag's beers are present. While I was chatting with Musser one day, the discussion turned to the aging of beers. He asked me if I'd be interested in owning the equivalent of about three cases of Christmas Ale, going back to 1982. He assured me they had been properly stored, and I graciously accepted. A couple of weeks later, we met again and the swap was made. Because Anchor alters the recipe for Christmas Ale each year and keeps those changes a secret, it is difficult to compare the cellared editions to the originals. All I could hope for was a delicate aging, which it fortunately has done.

As peculiar as the concept of aging beers for decades may seem, my reserve hardly qualifies for any sort of record. In late 2006, 250 bottles of Ratcliffe Ale from Worthington's White Shield Brewery of England were found within the vaults of the company. A value hasn't been placed on them. The bottles were sealed with corks and stored in the dark at a cool temperature. One bottle was opened and tasted by a few connoisseurs, one of whom was quoted as saying, "It's amazing that beers this antique can still taste so delicious. Established wisdom would say beers this old should taste of vinegar, damp rags and Marmite (a yeast extract). Instead, it showed flavors of raisins and sultanas (a variety of grape), baked apple and honey. The 1869 Ratcliffe Ale is bright and luminous like an ancient Amontillado sherry and has a meaty character like smoked partridge with hints of molasses. It's amazing it tastes this good after 137 years."

New Jersey resident Greg Drusdow first was exposed to the concept of aging beers several decades ago and now has built an impressive inventory. He said, "I first started understanding that there were some beers that could actually use some time in the bottle when traveling through Europe on work from the mid-1970s into the late 1980s. I got introduced to storing beer at the long-gone Sun Pub on Lambs Conduit Street in London. They had a selection of beers from all over England, which I enjoyed immensely, but they introduced me to Courage Imperial Russian Stout that was vintage-dated on each bottle. I still have three 170-ml. Bottles remaining from the 1980 and 1981 vintages. The label states that it was originally brewed for Catherine II of Russia and that a two- or three-year-old vintage was drinkable and could be aged for even longer. I also kept Thomas Hardy's Ale, having a vintage date of 1981. The back label indicates that it will last for at least twenty-five years since it is bottled with its natural yeast. They suggest a storage temperature of fifty-five degrees Fahrenheit and proudly boast that it is the strongest beer in Britain."

What are the thoughts of the experts from the beer world on aging beer? Via the technological miracles of email and the old-fashioned telephone, I posed some questions to Garrett Oliver, brewmaster of Brooklyn and author of *The Brewmaster's Table;* Stan Hieronymous, editor of Realbeer.com and author of numerous books on beer; Don Russell, award-winning reporter, radio show host, and writer for the *Philadelphia Daily News;* Peter LaFrance, author of *Beer Basics: A Quick and Easy Guide;* and Rex Halfpenny, certified beer judge and publisher of the *Michigan Beer Guide.* I wanted a cross section of people from a range of perspectives in order to get a balanced approach to the concept of storing beers. Here is what they had to offer:

The notion of cellaring beers remains unfamiliar to many. What are some benefits to this concept?

Garrett Oliver: Especially in bottle-conditioned beers, flavors will evolve and marry. Hops will drop back and allow malt and fruit flavors to come forward. Belgian beers in particular may become more spicy and complex. Oxidation can produce sherryish notes that can be pleasant in some beers.

Don Russell: Cellaring beer is like a great surprise. I save so much beer, I never really know what I've got in my cellar. When friends come over, I usually just reach for whatever I have in my fridge. But when beer lovers stop in, it's fun to blow them away with, say, a five-year-old Samiclaus or two or three vintages of Bigfoot [Sierra Nevada Bigfoot Barleywine].

Rex Halfpenny: Besides greed and lust to hoard and possess what few others do not, cellaring beer provides a ready stock of my favorite beverages in a variety of styles to suit any occasion and food pairing.

Obviously there is a degree of risk associated with cellaring beers. What are some of those pitfalls?

Garrett Oliver: Most beers, especially filtered ones, will not benefit from cellaring and are at their best when they leave the brewery. Filtered strong beers, such as barleywines, may age well. Pitfalls include unpleasant oxidation effects because no one wants a sherryish pale ale, loss of hop bitterness and aroma, and the development of haze and overall staling.

Peter LaFrance: Pitfalls are the usual: light and temperature swings.

Rex Halfpenny: Some beers do better with further conditioning and some do not. So stock rotation is important. Sometimes one forgets to discover an oxidized beer or worse, a beer that was once great, rendered to uncharacteristic acidity or tartness due to biological instability. Then there is the problem of space.

Have you ever stored beers? If so, were you satisfied with the results?

Garrett Oliver: I have a small collection of barleywines from the mid-1980s. they are absolutely magnificent, which they would not have been when they were released. They are finer and more complex than the best tawny ports I've tasted and I've tasted some great ones.

Stan Hieronymous: I've been pleased more times than not. It's most fun when you can taste, for instance, a 1995 Sierra Nevada Bigfoot and a 1998 and a 2001. maybe they made it a little bigger one year, a little hoppier another, but you've also got things that have been going on for different amounts of time.

Don Russell: I'm not always satisfied with the results, but that's my own damn fault. It usually has to do with huge temperature changes, like the time I discovered a little-used beer fridge in the garage had conked out for a month in the middle of July. I lost at least two years' worth of Rochefort on that one.

Rex Halfpenny: I always have far more beers in the cellar than I will ever drink without the help of friends. I love to get beers that will cellar and by that I mean those big, dark, high-alcohol, high-hops, big bottles, rare vintages, et cetera. The results are that I have lots of beers that will cellar well.

Name one beer you have cellared, how long it aged, and the effect on flavor.

Garrett Oliver: I have been asked to preside at vertical tastings of both Brooklyn Black Chocolate Stout at 8.7 percent ABV and Brooklyn Monster Ale at 10.7 percent. Black Chocolate Stout became smoother and more integrated over time. It also became drier and fruitier. The years tasted were 1994, 1995, 1996, 1997, 1998, and 1999. A New York bar, The Blind Tiger, once put five years of Monster Ale on draft; the Five-Headed Monster, they called it. This beer also became smoother over time. Beers that been somewhat hot and alcoholic at release had calmed and mellowed. Flavors were better integrated and the beers were fruitier and more complex.

Stan Hieronymous: Not the oldest or biggest, but the 1995 King & Barnes Christmas Ale at five years was still a masterpiece. But maybe it wasn't worth the bother because it was also great at a year, although it did take on more caramel notes and a light, delicate spiciness, considering it is brewed with no spices.

Don Russell: Like most, I go for heavy beers . . . barleywines, some of the Trappists, an occasional stout. Two of my favorites were Sam

Adams Triple Bock, which completely mellowed out after about three years, like a port; and De Dolle's Stille Nacht, which I thought turned kind of peppery over the course of four or five years. That reminded me of good sipping whiskey.

Peter LaFrance: I have kept three bottles well wrapped in the coolest northern-facing closet. One was a homebrewed Russian Imperial Stout that was kept for ten years. The carbonation was evident, the flavors were smooth with an almost cognac or port flavor, heavy with tart cherries, anise, and raspberry. It was very full-bodied, but the relatively high alcohol content kept it from tasting and feeling like molasses in the mouth. I also have a bottle of Thomas Hardy's Ale 1986 and Chimay Grand Reserve bottles in May, 1993. I'm waiting for the right moment to open them.

Rex Halfpenny: Alaskan Smoked Porter ages nicely, but loses smoke intensity. I have made an excellent, award-winning Export Scotch Ale that began to show instability by revealing sourness. Sierra Nevada Bigfoot is big, dark, and alcoholic, but oxidizes after a few years, though I still have and drink vintages as far back as the 1980s. J. W. Lees Harvest Ale is a great bottle-conditioned English barleywine, and some vintages age wonderfully by becoming slightly drier and more complex with a more rounded and fuller profile. This beer on wood [barrel-aged] is even better.

In conclusion, what advice would you have for the novice who is thinking about laying down some beers?

Garrett Oliver: Do not bother to age filtered beers with strengths of less than 7.5 percent by volume. They are unlikely to improve in any way. Bottle-conditioned beers with an alcohol by volume as low as 5 percent can age well, though not for more than a year. Strength tends to confer aging potential. Do not attempt to age beer at temperatures below forty-five degrees in the refrigerator as it will be a waste of time. Also, do not store aging beers at temperatures above seventy-five degrees for any period of time. A cellar, if you're lucky enough to have one, is best. An old refrigerator can be used as an aging cellar. Many old fridges are thrown out because they no longer get cold enough. These are perfect for storing beer in. Perfect temperatures will be in the fifty-to-sixty-degree range.

Stan Hieronymous: Label the bottles when you bought the beer and when you lay it down. Small price stickers from an office supply store work great. You might end up with a 1992 Thomas Hardy you've owned since then and a four-pack you found in a cooler last year. Monitor your stash. Obviously you have to have more than a single bottle on hand to do this, but taste the beer periodically. If a beer starts to drift on you, drink it while you can still enjoy it. Take good notes every time you taste a beer, when you lay it down, when you try the first bottle, et cetera. Pay particular attention to how the hop character changes, what yeast and malt flavors come to the fore, and if any spices are present. Consider a beer fridge if you don't have a basement. Get a temperature controller and keep the beer at fifty-eight degrees or so. Try to keep the beer as far from the compressor as possible. Too much shaking will confuse the heck out of any yeast in the bottle.

Don Russell: Date your beers with a marker. I forget to do this all the time, but there's no way you can remember what you have over time. Also, share your bottles with someone. It's fun and it's a great way to compare notes on how the tasting went.

Rex Halfpenny: There are rules. Dark and cool is primary. Second, dark color and high alcohol, followed by firm hops, will help the beer keep. Ales do better than lagers. Only unpasteurized and unfiltered beer will keep and improve. Some high-alcohol dark beers like EKU 28, Samiclaus, Eisbock, and the like will keep cool and dark, but not improve. Belgian lambics and gueuze will keep a few years and gain complexity.

Cascade hops are grown primarily in the Pacific Northwest and are popular in ales and lagers. They add a citrus, spicy flavor and aroma to beer, in addition to bitterness.

Beer derives its color to a major degree because of the roasting of the grain.
PHOTO: MICHAEL FELDMAN

Beer can come in a range of colors, mainly as a result of the grain used. Some beers use adjuncts, such as fruit or vegetables, which also give a distinct look.
PHOTO: MICHAEL FELDMAN

Sorbet can be complemented by drizzling a bit of fruit lambic.
PHOTO: MICHAEL FELDMAN

Certain beers give a distinct layer of foam when poured, depending upon the malt used. In general, wheat-based beers have the longest lasting bubbles. Be aware that the glassware also influences the retention of foam. Any soap residue will eliminate bubbles.
PHOTO: MICHAEL FELDMAN

Beers that are unfiltered retain yeast, a prime source of B vitamins. Those beers, typically wheat-based, will appear cloudy. Retention of the yeast adds to the flavor profile sought by the brewer. Although filtering can make for an aesthetically more pleasing beer, it alters the taste.
PHOTO: MICHAEL FELDMAN

The "Dream Team" Case of Beer

(See chapter 6)

Alaskan Smoked Porter

Anchor Steam

Avery the Reverend

Ayinger Celebrator

Brooklyn Local 1

Chimay Grand Reserve Blue

Czechvar

Dogfish Head Midas Touch
Golden Elixir

Kona Longboard
Lager

Duvel

Lindemans Framboise

Melbourn Brothers Strawberry
PHOTO: MICHAEL FELDMAN

Orval   Rodenbach   Rogue Shakespeare
               Grand Cru   Stout

Saison Dupont

Samuel Adams Chocolate Bock

Samuel Adams Utopias

Samuel Smith's Nut Brown Ale

Schneider Weisse

Sierra Nevada Pale Ale

Stone Arrogant Bastard Ale

Unibroue la Fin du Monde

Westmalle Trappist

5

TWENTY THINGS YOU ALWAYS WANTED TO KNOW ABOUT BEER, BUT DIDN'T KNOW WHO TO ASK

Throughout my travels, I meet a lot of people who want to talk about beer. Invariably, questions are asked, many of which are repeated. First and foremost, people want to know if I need an assistant. At this point I don't; fortunately there is no shortage of applicants waiting in the wings.

Second, there are those who want to know how I got started in this business. How people end up doing the things they do can be a complex journey. It's the rare person who decides at an early age what his calling in life might be. I doubt if too many kids decide to go into the beverage industry, although I do suppose some dabble in it in certain ways (wink).

I work as a full-time computer teacher. As such, my schedule allows me to have a couple of months away from the classroom each summer. Of course, that's time without a paycheck. Many in my profession hold second jobs, and some are preparing themselves for life after education. I tried different things back in the 1980s. I created personalized children's books for a brief while, investing plenty of money but seeing little return. I served as a computer consultant for a couple of years and worked on a delivery truck for one summer. Nothing gave me satisfaction. Then, for Christmas of 1991, the father of one of my students gave me a book about beer, written by Michael "The Beer Hunter" Jackson. I should mention that the parent and I had known each other since we were teenagers, thus he knew of my love for the beverage. Upon browsing through the book, my first words were, "You mean you can have a career writing about beer?" If it were only so easy.

I approached the editor of my local newspaper and asked if he might be interested in running a column that reviewed an upcoming beer festival in Pennsylvania. I proposed giving him a thousand words and a few pictures and ended my offer by saying that, if he liked it, he

The legendary "Beer Hunter," as I toured breweries with him several years ago. No one person influenced the cause of artisan beers more than Mr. Jackson. I was asked to participate in a brief filming while visiting with Mr. Jackson several years ago. The result was a documentary on him, released during the end of 2010. It was called "Beer Hunter: The Movie."

could use it for free. The piece ran and I was offered a monthly column with the paper at the rate of twenty-five dollars per article.

From there, I contacted the publisher of free monthly newspapers. You've probably seen them at community stores and restaurants. I did that for a couple of years, but continued to communicate with those in charge of publications that had a larger readership. Eventually, more doors opened for me. I've been having the time of my life since 1993, when that first column appeared in print.

When you're attempting to learn about any subject, there are various avenues that you should explore. In today's age, the Internet is a wonderful source for information, but there also is a good amount of false material continually being posted. Anyone can be "published" these days, with blogs being accepted as gospel. Regardless of the subject being researched, approach what you read with caution, unless you know the source. In my world, I looked to certain writers for guidance, including Mr. Jackson, Stephen Beaumont, Roger Protz, and a few others.

Most well-stocked bookstores will carry a couple of decent magazines, such as *Beer Connoisseur* and *All About Beer*. Columns tend to be insightful and well written, but beer-related news can be dated.

Then there are the beer newspapers, also called "beeriodicals" or "brewspapers." At the front of the list are *Ale Street News, Celebrator,* and the *Brewing News* family of publications, separated by geographic region (Mid-Atlantic, Southwest, and Great Lakes, for example). These papers generally are released bimonthly. Articles and features are, for the most part, written by those people who just like good beer. Almost all write for a very limited fee, but do so because of their love of the subject. Small breweries love these journals because they offer them a way to get the word out at no cost to them. Many of these microbreweries maintain little or no advertising budget, relying upon word of mouth or small newspapers to receive needed publicity. You'll note articles specific to parts of the country, allowing the reader the option of seeking a new beer release or possibly attend a festival in their area.

Although there is a subscription price to these newspapers, you can easily receive them for free by visiting your local brewery or brewpub. I've seldom seen one that didn't stock them and make them accessible at no cost.

Given the above, nothing beats speaking with someone who is passionate about a topic. I look forward to speaking with people about beer. I've gone to packaged goods stores, worked my way to the beer section, and spent the better part of an hour just discussing and recommending certain beverages . . . whether my information was needed or not, I suppose. It's just a character flaw.

In my years of teaching and speaking at beer tastings, I guess I've developed a talent at identifying when a person has a craving to know something but is a bit shy about asking. At my seminars, I can classify the attendees into certain groups. Most are curious about the "new breed" of flavors being released all the time. They think that all beer tastes pretty much the same, but know there is something going on that might be worth investigating.

There are others, normally no more than a quarter of those in audience, who have moved into the world of fine beers and want to zero in on a few brands that might be new or possibly acquire additional information about a favorite. And, of course, there typically is one person who has traveled extensively and has tasted certain beers from really small microbreweries. They also offer much to the presentation and to my personal knowledge.

As I said at the beginning of this section, many of the same questions are asked of me at the events I attend, so let's focus on some of the most popular.

Why are dark beers so heavy?
Heaviness is subjective. I've heard so many people contrast two popular beers, Coors Light and Guinness, by stating that Coors goes down easy but Guinness is just too substantial to enjoy.

Much of this relates to the presentation of each beverage. Go to your favorite pub and order a pint of each. If done properly, it will take substantially longer for you to receive your Guinness than the Coors Light. It's customarily dispensed by use of nitrogen as opposed to carbon dioxide and served at a warmer temperature, about fifty degrees or so, than is Coors. Nitrogen tends to render small, dense bubbles, the reason for the thick, creamy layer of foam that resides atop the pint. That's not something you're likely to find with Coors.

Much, but not all, color is generated by the type of grain(s) used. Dark grains can impart a roasted flavor, fooling the sense of taste into thinking the liquid is full and rich. We call that "mouthfeel." So you are kind of being fooled by color, carbonation, and flavor.

Check the alcohol content of the two beers and you'll find they are practically identical. Both come in at just a tad above 4 percent alcohol by volume (ABV).

Speaking of Guinness, how do they reproduce the tiny, compact bubbles in the can? There seems to be some sort of device inside.
Draught Guinness does have something inside its container, a little plastic gadget with the creative name of "widget." During canning, a mix of carbon dioxide and nitrogen is added. Because nitrogen is not as effervescent as "normally" carbonated beers, you'd have practically no head without the widget—the carbon dioxide would stay dissolved. The nitrogen dissolves and pressurizes the can. As the pressure increases, liquid is pushed into the little hole within the widget, squeezing the nitrogen in the gadget.

Upon popping open the can, the pressure instantly plunges (you'll hear the *whoosh*). The gas inside the widget immediately forces the beer out the little hole. This release causes the dissolved carbon dioxide to form little bubbles that rise to the top of the beer, duplicating the appearance of beer discharged from a tap.

Is kegged beer better than bottled beer?
This depends upon the beer. In general, it's safe to say that drinking beer that is as fresh as possible is best. If you go to your favorite watering hole, you may not know how long that beer has been on tap. Some

beers, usually the popular varieties, have a quick turnaround time, so freshness will not be an issue. Certain craft flavors may not be as lucky. I've been to bars in which I've gone through the entire lineup of kegged beers before finally settling on a bottle instead.

Bottle-conditioned beers, those that are conditioned with a touch of added yeast, don't work as well on tap. Time helps condition the beers, though, and they can favorably evolve over months or years.

I'm thinking about getting into homebrewing. Is it easy or difficult getting started?
Thomas Jefferson, third president of the United States and an avid homebrewer, purportedly said, "Beer, if drank in moderation, softens the temper, cheers the spirit and promotes health."

Until 1979, if you wanted to buy beer, your choices were confined to a select few brands made by a small number of large breweries. Variety? There was plenty as long as you wanted a light-bodied, straw-colored lager style. Then, in February of that year, President Jimmy Carter signed a bill allowing anyone twenty-one years of age or older the option of brewing up to a hundred gallons of beer a year within his own home, as long as the beer is for personal consumption.

Invariably, the question of constitutionality is asked. Although beer now could be homebrewed, the particulars were turned over to the individual states, and there may remain a handful that still have not taken their anti-homebrewing ordinances off the books. You'll need to check with your state's agencies for a determination of legality.

You may be wondering why it took until 1979 to make the homebrewing of beer allowable. The answer goes back almost half a century earlier, to January 16, 1920, and the implementation of the Eighteenth Amendment (the Volstead Act) to the US Constitution, otherwise known as Prohibition. It was this "Noble Experiment," as President Herbert Hoover called it, that barred the making, trafficking, and transporting of intoxicating beverages. For thirteen years, it was illegal to produce any drink containing more than 0.5 percent alcohol. Unfortunately for the federal government, Prohibition was met with a good deal of public resentment and defiance. It was estimated that over thirty thousand speakeasies existed in New York City by 1929. Nationally, tens of millions of dollars were exchanged in illicit beer sales.

The Volstead Act didn't eliminate homebrewing. In fact, over seven hundred million gallons of beer were being made yearly by the end of the 1920s. Large breweries remained in business by making malt syrup and other items for the food industry. Curiously, these commodities could be used to make beer.

It was the stock market crash of late October 1929 that indirectly led to the reversal of the Eighteenth Amendment. As the economy soured and unemployment grew, public pressure mounted to legalize beer as a means to stimulate job growth. Franklin D. Roosevelt, a candidate for the American presidency, took up the cause and promised to revoke the amendment, if elected. Within two weeks of taking office, Roosevelt asked Congress for the "immediate modification of the Volstead Act, in order to legalize the manufacture and sale of beer." On April 7, 1933, it became lawful to produce beer once again.

It became known as "New Beer's Day." Sales were so brisk that many regions ran out of beer within hours. President Roosevelt received numerous deliveries of the beverage from brewery owners, thankful that their fermenters again were filled. The formal ratification of the Twenty-first Amendment took place on December 5, 1933.

So, 1933 marked the date by which people could make beer in their homes, right? During Prohibition, people continued making alcohol; that statement can't be denied. How good it tasted was subject to debate, however. What mattered most was whether the drink was potent. By 1933, the homebrewing of wine and/or beer should have been legalized. Wine, in fact, was included, but a stenographer's error caused the words *and/or beer* to be excluded from the Federal Register.

Through the next few years and during the period of World War II, food supplies were limited. Only a few breweries endured and the beer that was produced was low in alcohol and flavor. Men were fighting the war and the beer drinkers within the United States primarily were women. The climate was conducive to the growing of rice and corn, two components that could be used in the brewing of beer, albeit producing a superficial flavor.

Little changed well into the 1970s. Mass-marketing techniques had instilled the belief that beer should be straw-colored with little taste. There were fewer than fifty American breweries in existence and that number was diminishing. However, the customs brought by immigrants were fading and a grassroots movement was arising as people sought a return to earlier times. The only way to drink beer the way our ancestors did was to make it in our own houses. It was this impetus that gave birth to the rise of the "micro" or "craft" brewery.

Two events that furthered this swelling activity took place in California. Fritz Maytag, of appliance fame, purchased the Anchor Brewing Company in San Francisco and vowed to revive the Old World styles of brewing by creating new and different beers. Then, in 1976, the first microbrewery was born in Sonoma, California. Although the New Albion Brewery lasted only six years, it inspired scores of homebrewers to further their craft.

Standard equipment for homebrewing.

For the person interested in creating homebrewed beer, there are plenty of options. Brewing is in small amounts, generally five gallons at a time, yielding a couple of cases of twelve-ounce bottles. You'll need equipment necessary to handle the three principal steps of brewing: boiling, fermenting, and bottling. Start with a stainless-steel pot or kettle with a capacity of at least four gallons.

Next, get a five-gallon fermenter, called a carboy. Think of the large jugs that are used to hold springwater. The carboy will need to be secured with a lid, then fitted with a rubber stopper (called an air lock) with a hole from which a clear plastic hose is attached. This will allow the built-up carbon dioxide to escape while protecting the fermenter from airborne microorganisms that could pollute the developing beer.

Finally, get your bottles for packaging. To be safe, about fifty-five or sixty twelve-ounce bottles (or a couple dozen champagne bottles) should do the trick. As convenient as twist-off caps are, pry-off or "crowned" caps will seal better. As a result, you'll need either a handheld or bench-mounted capper.

This is how beer bottles were capped in the days prior to automation and is how a homebrewer might do things today.

Depending on where you live, obtaining these items should not be too troublesome. Many communities have homebrew supply shops where the ingredients, recipe books, and more can be purchased, generally for under a hundred dollars. Staff are knowledgeable and eager to help the novice as well as the seasoned brewer. Many stores offer brewing classes and unique events designed to increase awareness and bring more people into the hobby.

Homebrew clubs are springing up regularly in many locales. Formats and procedures vary. Some clubs have few members and meet informally. Others are large and dynamic, complete with periodic activities and competitions. All, however, welcome those ready and willing to develop their new interest in brewing.

Beer is made of four components: hops, yeast, a malted grain (usually barley, yielding fermentable sugars), and water. The first three may be obtained in varying styles, depending upon what you choose to brew. Most beginners favor packaged kits of malt extract, a syrupy concoction that may also include a container of yeast or added hops. Because this method is so simple, some neophytes shun the process—the decisions have already been made. The true hobbyist enjoys and welcomes having the flexibility to modify each batch she creates.

Consequently, some kits afford the homebrewer the luxury of working like a pro. Specialty grains are included, as are fresh hop pellets, designed to safeguard quality yet keeping the procedure relatively simple. Known as "extract brewing," this format will satisfy most people, initially producing a highly acceptable beverage.

In time, you might move into a more specialized area known as all-grain brewing. You will need more equipment and time to devote to the process, but the result will rival most commercially available brands.

There are those who would prefer not to make the investment in equipment for a hobby they may practice intermittently. That's a valid claim. Throughout the United States, Canada, and other countries, there are companies known as brew-on-premise, or BOP, that can take the apprehension out of brewing for the beginner and provide support for the more accomplished brewer.

The concept behind a BOP is simple. The customer creates a high-quality beer at the location of the enterprise. By renting the equipment and buying the supplies, time, space, and recipes, you receive firsthand assistance and expertise. Some BOPs offer wine, cider, or mead preparation as well. Plan on spending a few hours on your first visit as you make your own beer. Oh, don't forget to give your beer a name and original label design, which you will pick up when you return to bottle your finished product two weeks later. You'll walk away with a delicious beer that can be modeled after your favorite libation, coming in at a fraction of the price of what you would pay at your local retailer.

In central New Jersey, about seventy-five miles north of my home, is a BOP called The Brewer's Apprentice. Jo-Ellen Ford, one of the company's owners, said, "People who don't know homebrewing can find it somewhat intimidating. We take the fear out of it by trying to recognize the level of the person coming to visit and by making them feel comfortable in what they are doing." At The Brewer's Apprentice, you'll make six cases (seventy-two bottles) of twenty-two-ounce bottles. The fee is dependent on what is produced, although it is possible to have a cost per bottle in the neighborhood of two dollars.

An attractive aspect of brewing at a BOP is the fact that the customer is not responsible for setup or cleanup. During my last visit to The Brewer's Apprentice, all my equipment was ready as I met my scheduled appointment. What did I make? My daughter Kristin and I selected a holiday spiced beer called Kris-Mas Ale, based on an existing recipe in stock at the business, but altered somewhat to suit our palates.

Nothing is trouble-free. Things can go astray in any process. When you're homebrewing, cleanliness is of paramount importance. Bacterial contamination can quickly ruin what normally would be a flavorful beer. One way to determine if corruption has taken place is to examine the surface of the beer where it touches the bottle. The presence of sediment around the neck is an indicator of infestation.

Where did the problem originate? Bacterial sources can be found anywhere and everywhere, from your hands to the area on which you are doing your preparations. For this reason, it is mandatory that you

soak your bottles and fermenter in a solution of household chlorine
bleach and water. Then rinse with hot water.

The siphon hoses you use should not looked stained. Sanitize them
prior to handling and replace them when worn. Any plastic equipment
must be visually inspected. Scratches are ideal places for bacteria. As
your level of ability increases, so do the chances of off-flavors. That
topic is best addressed at another time, however.

*I heard about a festival where over two hundred different beers were
going to be served. What should I expect?*
One of the fastest-growing aspects of the specialty beer arena is festivals.
They're gushing onto the scene in virtually every state in this country;
most major cities play host to multiple events.

With huge profits to be made, promotional companies are coming
out of the woodwork to stage these labor-intensive happenings.
Conversely, many beer festivals are labors of love, produced by
breweries, enterprising beer aficionados, homebrew clubs, and craft
beer organizations. It seems as though everyone is jumping into the
fray with a new beer festival once they get wind of the big payoff. If
quaffing brew at such an event is in your future, take it from me you
need to be prepared. You'll not only be more comfortable, but also learn
more if you show up with the proper accessories and attire. Armed with
beer etiquette awareness, you'll heighten your enjoyment and wow your
friends with your suds savvy.

When you've decided on a beer festival you want to attend, purchase
your tickets in advance. They're usually less expensive in advance—but
there's nothing more disappointing than being turned away because
an event has sold out. Besides, it's a hassle cooling your heels in line to
purchase your ticket at the door when you're revved up for your first brew.

If you're taking public transportation, be sure to check the schedule
well in advance. And don't forget to check departure times; you wouldn't
want to be stranded at the corner instead of heading home because the
last train or bus departed at 11 PM and you arrived at the terminal at
11:05.

Oktoberfest is an annual two-and-a-half week festival held in Munich, Germany. Over five million people from all over the world attend. Only beers brewed within the city limits of Munich are eligible to be served at Oktoberfest. Approximately eight million pints are consumed during this event, first held in 1810.

A festival that I once attended was located in a large hall sitting above a parking garage. As attendees exited, there was but one way to turn. The end of the street featured seven police cars with lights flashing, just waiting to test the drivers for levels of intoxication. I would imagine the host city had a busy but profitable evening.

If you aren't taking public transportation, don't drive yourself. Treat a friend to a ticket in exchange for being a designated driver. I've noted that increasing numbers of promoters are offering discounted or free tickets to designated drivers. There's no need to feast before the show, but be sure to have some food in your stomach before beginning the tasting session to ease the impact of any lapse in judgment you may make in beer quantity.

Dress casually and wear nonbinding clothes—because after a day of suds sipping, you likely will experience bloating. Above all, wear comfortable hiking boots, walking shoes, or sport sandals. You'll be on your feet for most of the session, and concrete convention floors and asphalt parking lots are unforgiving surfaces. Shorts or jeans are fine as long as you've got plenty of pockets for carrying accessories. As for your shirt, bear in mind that there's a fair chance that you'll either spill some of your drink or have someone bump into you. Stout stains look unsightly on a white SAVE THE ALES T-shirt. If the event is alfresco, bring sunblock and ultraviolet ray-blocking polarized sunglasses that adjust to the changing light underneath or outside the beer tents.

Count on peddlers selling water at two dollars or more a pop, so think about bringing your own. This will be a welcomed, especially if you are outdoors in the hot sun. There should be plenty of photo opportunities should you bring a camera. Are you getting the impression that a backpack or some type of carrying bag is a good idea?

Pick up a festival program upon entry so you can map out your plan of attack. After all, you don't want to spend valuable time sampling bland or boring beer. Go for the good stuff. Begin with your "ten most wanted," list because your taste buds will lose their edge quickly. Don't forget to savor, not guzzle your beer, especially at the beginning when it really hits the spot. Scope out the locations of the restrooms and food court; if necessary, arrange for a rendezvous point for your friends and you.

Don't forget to bring a pen so you can take beer notes. I write directly on my program, but if you don't want to mark it up, bring a notepad. If you own any pocket guides to beer, they may come in handy for looking up information. In many cases, the program itself will offer descriptions of each beer served.

Many beer festivals offer very cool door and raffle prizes, so stash some extra cash for buying tickets. Plus, you may want to purchase some snacks, beer ware, or merchandise that you couldn't otherwise find. Earlier I mentioned wearing clothing with plenty of pockets. That's where you'll be carrying your bottle opener, cash, pen, notepad, program, pocket guide, and anything else to which you might want easy access.

Sorry to say this, but you should plan on waiting in line for some things like festival entry, toilet facilities, food, water, and beer. If the festival is well organized, the lines should be at a minimum. Pushing and shoving at beer booths never is acceptable. Likewise, after you've gotten your beer, move well away from the table so others can get their samples.

Expect to receive small servings of beer, usually two or three ounces each. The rules may vary from show to show, in accordance with the organizers or state laws. It may not seem like much, but it adds up to a lot of beer quaffing. If you are served a beer you don't like, don't hesitate to dump it. There usually are buckets at the serving tables for that purpose. Why get one step closer to your personal limit drinking marginal beers? A select few promoters offer tokens for each desired beer. In this scenario, you can expect to receive six-ounce-or-larger servings that you can split with friends if you'd like to sample more drinks through the course of the event.

Children are inappropriate at beer festivals and generally are prohibited from entering the area. Find a sitter or ask Mom or Dad to take care of them. This is an adult event and is not for families. Dogs are usually allowed at outdoor festivals (check before bringing Fido), but I've seen far too many animals suffer from heat prostration and sunburn from being led around on hot pavement by their unsuspecting masters.

Take a few minutes to ask questions of the brewery representatives or the brewer himself, if he's there. The more you learn about beer styles, the brewing process, and historical idiosyncrasies of beer and breweries, the richer and more fulfilling your beer experiences will be. The people with whom you'll speak will appreciate it, too, and may show you some extra courtesy and kindness. Of course, it goes without saying, but a please, a smile, and a thank-you or a compliment about a beer will go a long way with busy, tired volunteers and the serving team.

Once you've attended the festival and you feel up to it, evaluate your experience. Was your game plan a good one? Would you have done better to have visited the food court early before the lines developed? Did you bring your pocket guide but never look at it? At your next festival, use the strategies that worked and ditch the ones that didn't. Before you know it, you'll be a savvy beer explorer.

I bought a cold case of beer, but by the time I got home it was warm. Will this damage the flavor?
Temperature variations can be hazardous to a beer's health, but I wouldn't be overly concerned by one episode of cold to warm to cold. Having this occur frequently certainly affects freshness, and the flavor will be less than what you expected. Get the beer home and keep it in a constant cool temperature, hopefully removed from as much light as possible, and enjoy your purchase.

I bought a case of beer that tasted bad. Can I return it?
That's a complicated question that needs explanation. If I went to the supermarket and purchased a can of soup that I didn't like, should I be able to return it? In theory it sounds nice, but it's just not practical from a business standpoint. Not liking the flavor is an unacceptable reason for a store return. Conversely, buying a product that is defective should afford the customer the option of an exchange or refund. But how do you recognize a faulty beer as opposed to a flavor you don't fancy?

Some people feel that an overly bitter beer must be bad. Bitterness comes from hops, and the amount and type of hops influence that bitterness. There are beers on the market today that are very aggressive, in terms of that ingredient, by design. So bitterness can't truly be a mitigating element.

The level of carbonation also must be tossed aside as a warning sign. Carbonation will vary from style to style, and certain beers have almost no bubbles. There is a measure of truth to the theory that those beers with a high alcohol content, such as barleywines, have little carbonation. Completely flat beers are rare.

The presence of solid particles, sometimes called "floaties," is unattractive and unwanted, but not unhealthy. Don't mistake them for the cloudiness associated with an unfiltered beer (see below). Floaties are globs of protein that can occur when a bottled beer is old. They should be visible through the bottle. The taste may be compromised, so that may be reason for a return visit to your vendor. Floaties don't materialize often with domestic brands, especially those that have a brisk turnaround time.

Sourness is a prized trait in styles of beer such as those in the lambic family. You'll notice that quality in wheats, as well. Beers of this sort are an acquired taste, and if you're currently drinking light American pilsners, for example, you probably won't accept the drastic change in taste these beers present. If I bought a mass-marketed domestic lager, on the other hand, and picked up on sourness, I'd know the sample was infected.

Have you ever popped the top off a bottle only to release a gusher? It could signify a beer that has bacterial contamination. Why does this happen? In a bottle-conditioned beer, the yeast continues a little bit of fermentation within the bottle. If tainted, the bacteria will not stop their work, resulting in an escalation in pressure. If your bottle is corked, treat it as you might champagne and point it away from people. I once saw a cork poke a hole in a ceiling tile when released.

When you have a gusher, smell the contents. If you detect a vinegary aroma, well, it's probably bad. If there is no offensive odor, take a sip and, if it's satisfactory, go with it.

A common description for beer that is past its prime is that the liquid is "skunky." Sounds appetizing, huh? Exposure to light can cause this foul sensation. Don't worry, it's highly noticeable.

Exposure to oxygen can cause off-flavors of wet cardboard, mustiness, or sherry. What a cross section, to say the least! In aged beers, the latter trait can be enjoyable; in others it is offensive. Return it.

I once attended a beer festival in which a specific brand of a noted brewer's beer tasted of butter. Butter and butterscotch taste good and sometimes are desirable, but they're an indication of a by-product of fermentation and are not how the beer is intended to taste. Low levels are not necessarily bad, but higher ones point to a beverage that is defective.

Another form of bacterial infection is DMS or dimethyl sulfide. Your beer will smell like shellfish or cooked vegetables. I've seen evidence of this in quite a few homebrews.

Also common to homebrews are phenols from fermentation. The beer will smell like an adhesive bandage or possibly medicinal or clovey. You must be aware of the style of beer, as certain wheat-based beers are intended to have this trait. In others, though, it is a sign of bacterial infection.

Doesn't beer make you fat?

The culprit is the calories coming from alcohol. But there are calories in almost everything you drink. Think of the last time you were at a bar. There's a good chance there were munchies present, probably chips, peanuts, pretzels, and the like. What do they have in common? Fat, salt, and calories. Try eating just one peanut.

Look at the person's lifestyle before blaming beer for causing a weight problem. Is that person sedentary or active? At a recent speaking engagement, one member of the audience asked, "You must not drink much beer. You're not overweight." I'm six feet tall and weigh 180 pounds. Of course, moderation is the key, as it is with anything. I average anywhere from one to three beers daily.

Stew Smith is a former Navy SEAL and current writer who appeared with me on *Beer Radio,* previously heard on the Sirius Satellite Radio Network. Stew offered the following advice: "There is no reason why you cannot have six-pack abs and still drink a six-pack a week. Once again, excessive beer drinking is not recommended by anyone in the health industry. If you simply enjoy drinking beer and are serious about your health, moderation in drinking alcohol and eating good foods, combined with habitual daily exercise, is your ticket to reaching your goals."

Alcohol contains no fat or cholesterol, although the nutritional value is dependent upon the type of drink. For my money, I'll stick with beer. In its simplest form, it contains only water, hops, yeast, and grain.

Aren't low-calorie or light beers just watered down?

The concept behind reduced-calorie beers had its start around World War II when breweries attempted to attract women. By the 1970s, there were only a few dozen breweries left in the United States, and most made the same bland stuff. I'm not going to say that low-alcohol versions never were solely diluted. In fact, there was one brewer who, in his six-pack, packaged five bottles of his "regular" brew along with one bottle of carbonated water, asking people to make their own.

The construction of a low-alcohol beer can take as much effort as that given to any other variety. Raw beer is called wort (pronounced *wert*). It's thinned in the fermenter, but the addition of yeast leads to different flavors and a lower alcohol content.

Some breweries add enzymes to the wort to break down the sugars. Altering the fermentation or adding rice or corn will provide cheap fermentables, but will produce what essentially is a tasteless product, rather high in calories. What happens then is that watering down takes place. So, the question does have a degree of truth.

The first light beer was actually produced in the late 1960s at the Rheingold brewery. The creator of Gablinger's Diet Beer, the late Dr. Joseph L. Owades, once said, "I asked people why they didn't drink beer. The answer I got was twofold. 'One, I don't like the way beer tastes. Two, I'm afraid it will make me fat.' It was a common belief then that drinking beer made you fat. People weren't jogging and everybody believed beer drinkers got a big, fat beer belly. Period. I couldn't do anything about the taste of beer, but I could do something about the calories."

The formula for light beer ended up being used as Meister Brau Lite. Miller Brewing later bought Meister Brau, tweaked the blueprint just a bit, and rebadged the beer a few years later as Miller Lite. Bring in a snappy advertising campaign that included actors, comedians, and athletes and you had a breakaway beer in the mid-1970s.

Isn't a beer served in a frozen mug the best?
It is if you don't want much flavor. Then again, many mass-marketed and low-alcohol brands lack intense flavor. Think of the leftovers from the meal you had the night before. When you go to your fridge and eat it, the flavor intensity just isn't the same because the food isn't at the ideal serving temperature. The flavor of most well-constructed beers emerges at milder temperatures. Also, as the ice from a frozen mug melts, you are diluting your drink.

I saw a layer of something in the bottom of my bottle. Has it gone bad?
If it's a bottle-conditioned beer, probably not. As was stated earlier, the substance you see is yeast, added prior to bottling to continue the fermentation process. You can deal with this in a couple of ways. When pouring, you can simply decant the liquid, leaving those last few ounces. Or you may opt to gently swirl the bottle, letting the yeast blend a bit.

Remember that those final couple of ounces will look and taste different from your initial pour. When I'm serving a bottle-conditioned beer at a formal tasting, I attempt to mix the yeast in the bottle; otherwise I omit serving that final pour.

Yeast is nothing more than B vitamins, making it a very healthy drink. If the concept of bottle-conditioned beers is foreign to you, I suggest drinking those last couple of ounces to see if the taste appeals to you. Be aware that the beer will appear murkier than the initial glass you served; if aesthetics matter, you may not be impressed. By the way, bottle-conditioned beers should be labeled as such.

If you are drinking a filtered beer and see solids, I'd be concerned. You probably have a relic that should be tossed aside.

Is it true that bock beer is produced when they clean the bottom of the barrel?
This story has been going around for decades; it's one of the first I heard, long before I got into this industry. Nothing could be farther from the truth. This style of beer, German in origin, comes from the

German word that refers to a goat. That's why you'll often see images of that animal on a bottle's label.

Bock beers are strong lagers, richer and somewhat darker in color because of the amount of grain used.

Should a wedge of lemon be served with a glass of wheat beer?
I believe the practice of adding a slice of lemon or lime started in Germany in the 1960s and spread to this country some twenty years later. Although there are some who wouldn't have their beer served in any other manner, I opt to drink without it. A hefeweizen or a Belgian wit already has elements of citrus and spices in it; I don't want the aroma and flavor altered in a way the brewer didn't intend. Also, adding citrus is one good way to wipe out any foam, one of the attractive components in a wheat beer.

What I strongly object to is when a bartender serves a wheat beer with the wedge added before asking if that's how the customer wants it.

How about the addition of fruit to the brew? It seems strange, but I'm noticing more of these beers being sold.
During the colonial era of this country, brewers used anything that would provide yeasts to perform their magic. Many times, this meant using locally grown produce in lieu of imported barley, an item that was heavily taxed. There is documentation going back to 1771 of commercial recipes that include parsnips, spruce, and pumpkins.

Although some of the early beermaking recipes look a bit strange by modern-day standards, items like corn and molasses were staples; to this day, most large breweries continue to use corn as an inexpensive way to augment production. A brewer once told me, "Most good beer should be made with barley, in the same way that good hamburgers are all beef. Barley is expensive, and the more fillers that are used, the bigger the profits."

Fruit beers are what the name implies: beverages with fruit and herbs added during the brew. Years ago, the use of fruit to enhance flavor was common even before hops were found to be a preservative for the drink.

At virtually any brewery, the decision to use produce in the mix is subject to the decision of the brewer and the type of beers desired. Tom Baker, owner and brewer of Earth, Bread & Brewery in Philadelphia, the now-defunct Heavyweight Brewing, once developed a brew that he identified as Ch-Chuck. No, he doesn't have a speech impediment; rather, Ch-Chuck was the second iteration of a beer once called Chuck (named because he "chucked" various ingredients into the concoction). Ch-Chuck picked up where the original left off based on the inclusion of twenty pounds of sour cherries and the juice into the fermenter.

Another brewer took a recipe developed as a homebrewer and transferred it to his brewery. Chocolate Cherry Imperial Stout was a beer that used Hershey's cocoa in the boil with cherry puree added. That brewer said, "This is something I wanted to do professionally. I do believe, however, that fresh fruit should be used whenever possible, instead of extract, which gives an artificial taste."

Not all breweries opt for fruit-infused beer. One West Coast brewer told me, "I just don't want to brew with fruit. Plus, I don't like to brew what I don't drink."

When looking for a fruit beer, you may find the words *kriek* (cherry), *framboise* (raspberry), and *pêche* (peach), as these are three of the most common fruits used.

Other fruits are used in brewing, as well. You can find some tasty beers with blueberries, cranberries, apricots, black currants, strawberries, pears, apples, and more. During autumn, there are several remarkable pumpkin beers to be found. And now, these beers are being produced worldwide.

Fruit beers make invigorating aperitifs. If you're pairing foods, consider chocolate desserts, tangy cheeses, mussels, and salads in a fruit-based dressing. Alcohol content may vary, but the upper limit of most of these beverages seldom exceeds 6.5 percent alcohol by volume.

They may not be for everyone, but many people find fruit beers to be unique and refreshing. And they just may change your perception about this old, yet complex drink, originally built from just a handful of ingredients.

Organic foods are everywhere. Will we ever see organic beer?
Look no farther than the shelves of your favorite beer vendor. Organics are here and are doing very well, thank you. But first, let's define what it means to be organic.

In the late 1990s, the US Department of Agriculture developed the National Organic Program to regulate and inspect food and beverage products that seek the claim of being organic. This program states that "before a product can be labeled 'organic,' a Government-approved certifier inspects the farm where the food is grown to make sure the farmer is following all the rules necessary to meet USDA organic standards." There is no claim, of course, that organically prepared items are safer or more nutritious than those commercially prepared. As it applies to the making of beer, the grains and hops used must be grown and handled without any toxic chemical inputs. To then be certified as organic, the fields where barley or wheat (for example) are grown are done, as well as of production and processing area. Regular soil and water testing may occur to make certain that benchmarks are being met.

Adhering to the strict standards demanded by the program is not easy and takes time and money. Consequently, there exist beers on the market today that probably are organic; they just can't advertise as such. But the demand for food and beverages of this ilk is growing at a feverish rate, far exceeding the growth of traditional beer sales.

Probably the most recognizable name in organic beer is that of Wolaver, owner of the popular Otter Creek Brewing Company. Certified as using at least 98 percent organic ingredients, Wolaver's can be found in most, but not all states. As for flavors, the company has a wide array, brewing a wheat, an India pale ale, a brown ale, and an oatmeal stout, among others.

In England, the Samuel Smith Old Brewery at Tadcaster makes an Organic Ale and Organic Lager. Both are certified by the National Organic Program. You'll appreciate the serving size, as both come in 18.7-ounce Yorkshire pint bottles.

Jon Cadoux is the founder of the Peak Organic Brewing Company in Portland, Maine, a brewery that was unveiled in 2006. He was quoted as saying, "We believe that using barley and hops that are grown without toxic and persistent pesticides and chemical fertilizers makes our beer tastier and more enjoyable, both for you and the planet." He initially released three flavors: pale ale, nut brown ale, and amber ale. All are extremely flavorful.

The claim that organically constructed beer tastes better is subjective, although a representative from a brewery making these beers said the following: "There are no chemical residues to get in the way of fermentation. My people feel that using a grain free of pesticides leads to cleaner brewing traits, leading to a more complete drawing out of sugars."

The movement to organics has caused Anheuser-Busch to get into the game. You may have seen a couple of its beers packaged under the Wild Hop and Stone Mill labels. Try to find the name *Budweiser* on those bottles, I dare you.

There are a few revolutionary brewers who are moving to the forefront of the movement, but the success of organic beers will depend on several factors, including concern for the planet and, of course, flavor.

Why aren't microbrewed beers canned?

That's not a bad question! An increasing number of breweries are doing just that, realizing that canned beer offers certain advantages over bottled. One obstacle that needed to be overcome was the leaching of a metallic taste into the beer, a valid consideration. Nowadays, cans are lined with a water-based polymer that protects the beverage from the metal. Although there can be other reasons why canned beer might taste tinny, it should not be because of the process itself.

Think of the advantages that cans have over bottles. First is cost. Manufacturing a can costs less than does making a bottle. Any savings to the brewer can help the consumer. Cans are easy to carry and less likely to break than bottles.

There are places that allow the sale and use of cans, as opposed to bottles. In fact, there are numerous public places that have outlawed bottles for various reasons.

What destroys beer? Your first response should be exposure to light. Need any more be said about the benefits of canning?

There are a couple of other factors to consider. One is image. A generalized statement would suggest that the typical craft beer drinker purely expects her beer in a bottle, equating cans with those beers from the large breweries. Well, that's slowly changing. The Colorado-based Oskar Blues Brewery has been marketing its Dale's Pale Ale and Old Chubb Scottish Ale in cans and is enjoying a successful run. I've had both and can honestly state they are fine beers.

Sly Fox Brewery, with multiple locations in Pennsylvania, now is selling more beer in cans than in bottles, in part based on customer interest. Adding this aspect of packaging has led to double-digit increases in annual sales. The fact that brewer Brian O'Reilly's beer is damn good doesn't hurt, either.

Initially, I had to deal with the visual impact of a can and the mental image of what is inside. Unfortunately, I've noticed a few retailers restricting these beers to the bottom shelf, far from eye level, an area that tends to decrease sales.

Barrier number two involves the current state of bottling. Notice the amount of beers that are being presented in large bottles, those 750ml monsters that once were thought to be reserved for wines. Appearance is important to many brewers, who take pride in how their bottles look, including label design. Browse through the aisles at your liquor retailer and look at vodka bottles, for example. Many are beautifully shaped and constructed. It kind of reminds me of the days when record albums were sold and I bought one solely on how it looked.

I've not seen beer bottles offered in terribly unusual shapes yet, nor do I feel that this is likely to happen at anytime soon. Then again, never say never.

Exposure to light damages bottled beer. So how do you buy beer from a store that obviously is lighted?

One of the most common concerns people have about buying of beer in bottles is spoilage. Everyone has his own ideas as to how to reduce that risk, but certain facets are unavoidable. Much is made of the color of a beer bottle. It's believed that the darker the bottle, the less likely it is that the contents will be jeopardized by ultraviolet rays. You are likely to find bottles that are shaded amber or green, or are clear; most are amber. Why the differences? Mostly because of marketing. Miller Brewing, for example, is associated with clear bottles; Heineken is correlated with green. I've heard it said that green or clear bottles will cause the beer to turn bad more quickly than amber and I've seen data that support that claim. Yet decades ago, patents were issued to create light-protective green glass, a process that can block or reduce damaging rays. Furthermore, some companies have worked with the hops included in the brewing recipe to make their products more stable when exposed to light. More recently, Beck's introduced a clear glass bottle that protects the beer from light. During processing, the glass is tailored to improve its light-absorption qualities, better defending against flavor changes.

Another key is in whether the beer you are buying is pasteurized. Most beer is pasteurized, and that process helps prevent unwanted changes from transpiring quickly. Again, remember that many craft beers are unpasteurized and unfiltered, meaning they are susceptible to unwelcomed variations.

Here is how I attempt to partially get around the artificial lighting concern. When buying beer, I do not take the package that sits at the front of the shelf; I opt for the second or third one. It's likely to be a bit more in the dark and receives less direct light.

I had a bottle of [fill in the name of a non-American brewed beer] in [fill in the name of a country other than the United States] and it tasted much better there than here. Why is that the case?
I hear this one all the time. There is no plot to offer cheaper and better versions of beer outside America. Differing versions of certain beers are sold, however. Take Guinness, for example, a beer that frequently is found on tap and in restaurants. There are assorted types of this brand produced and distributed worldwide. Are you familiar with Guinness Foreign Extra Stout, Guinness Red, Guinness Special Export Stout,

and Guinness Bitter? You are if you're an extensive traveler or have special friends who bring these beers back for you.

Usually this concern arises when you've found that great beer you love while at the Caribbean Islands. It just wasn't as good here. Of course, at the time you were sitting on the beach on a sunny eighty-five-degree day, enjoying a relaxing vacation. You drank your next bottle at home when the kids were fighting and you'd just found out your checking account was overdrawn. Similar scenarios?

We can even apply this to domestic beers. Let's use the Boston Beer Company, makers of the Samuel Adams lineup of beers, as an example. If you think their entire portfolio was brewed in Boston, check again. Sam Adams is produced in several American cities, including Cincinnati. Think of Coors and its "Rocky Mountain Spring Water," a wonderful marketing campaign. In some parts of the country, buying a Coors product was difficult, going back thirty years or so. Elitism developed. Then Coors opened a plant in Virginia. The Rocky Mountain water? Well, it's somewhat true. The beer was shipped eastward in a highly concentrated form, then blended with local water to reduce costs.

Why do the British drink warm beer?
They don't, but compared with Americans, you might make a case for that assumption. Most domestic drinkers prefer their beverages ice-cold, with the exception of those who have made the move into the world of more flavorful brews. In much of Western Europe, cask-conditioned beer is popular—meaning beer that has undergone a second fermentation in a cask (somewhat like a keg). Because yeast is added, fermentation of remaining sugar continues, resulting in the release of some carbon dioxide and a progression of flavor development. The practice of serving cask ales is becoming more prevalent in the United States. There now are brewpubs and bars that sporadically offer cask nights. Philadelphia's Grey Lodge Pub hosts an event referred to as "Friday the Firkinteenth." This somewhat quirky title reflects a happening that only takes place on a Friday the thirteenth of a month.

The Grey Lodge
Pub in Philadelphia
was recently named
by Beer Advocate
as one of the top
50 bars in the
USA. When a
month has a Friday
the 13th, the Pub
breaks out the cask
conditioned ales,
no less than 25
per session!

On that date, casks of different beers are available for sampling. Fans of
the Grey Lodge anxiously check their calendars near the beginning of
each year and schedule their pilgrimages to this extremely popular site.
Incidentally, a firkin is a quarter of a barrel and is considered the norm
for serving cask ales.

Is barleywine considered beer or wine?
The biggest, boldest, and baddest of all beer styles is barleywine, a
beer that often reaches the double-digit level in alcohol. Originating
in England around 1900, barleywine is fermented and derived from
grain and not fruit, making it a beer. The "wine" portion of the style
comes from the fact that the beer is about as strong as wine. These
beers conventionally show themselves during winter months and are
meant for sipping. Carbonation is relatively modest.

Barleywines are fruity and warming, great to sip after a meal or while sitting before a fire. The color can range from amber to dark brown. English versions tend to be sweeter and less alcoholic than their American counterparts, but all are fine candidates for cellaring. Like wines, some barleywines are perfectly acceptable for years from bottling.

The naming of barleywines seems to inspire resourcefulness at some breweries. Here's a representative sample: Sierra Nevada Bigfoot, Anchor Old Foghorn, Dogfish Head Immort Ale, Horn Dog, Insanity, and Old Knucklehead.

I was reading the menu of beers made at my local brewpub and saw columns labeled ABV *and* IBU. *What are they?*
ABV stands for "alcohol by volume"; IBU refers to "international bittering units." Stated as a percentage, ABV gives the drinker an idea of the amount of alcohol in a particular drink. The tricky part is in recognizing whether the figure is listed as "by volume" or "by weight" (ABW). There's a difference. If you know the former, multiply that number by 0.8 and you'll get a good approximation of the measurement by weight. Conversely, taking the alcohol by weight and multiplying it by 1.25 will give you a good idea of the alcohol by volume. For example, a beer that comes in at 5 percent ABW, multiplied by 1.25, will equal a 6.25 percent ABV beer. To compute "proof," commonly used with spirits, double the ABV. A 13 percent barleywine is 26 proof.

It's a shame there is no standard for reporting the amount of alcohol in a beer, nor is there a law requiring breweries to do so. Apparently, the stance of the government is that labeling how much alcohol is in a certain beer would encourage drinkers to look for the strongest beverage. Personally, I feel that knowing beforehand what I am about to drink is valuable, especially if I plan on driving. I recall attending a beer dinner in the early 1990s in which six beers were served and all registered at least 9 percent ABV. No bottles were labeled as such, nor did the host identify these valuable numbers to the diners. By the end of the evening, he had a room of very happy people, many of whom were, unfortunately, taking to the roads.

IBU is a generalized view of how bitter a beer may be, because of the presence of hops. This number can be a bit misleading, however. A low-alcohol American lager can have an IBU reading as low as 5; an India pale ale can reach 65, and certain barleywines, especially those made in the United States, can reach 100. But would you say that the barleywine tastes more bitter than the IPA? Probably not. The deciding factor is in the amount of malt used. Remember that barleywines have an elevated amount of alcohol when compared with an India pale ale. Without a much higher quantity of added hops, the beer would taste syrupy sweet and be unpalatable. So if you're using IBUs to determine of a beer's bitterness, be certain to compare it with its ABV or ABW.

Occasionally you may see another set of letters attached to a beer: OG or "original gravity." Sometimes this is called "starting gravity" or even "specific gravity." If you are having a flashback to your high school chemistry class and feeling a bit stressed, please relax. Here's all you need to know. Water has an original gravity of 1.000. A developing beer's original gravity will be higher than that of water because it contains more fermentable and unfermentable materials. In other words, it's denser or heavier than water. After fermentation is completed, the starting number will drop close to that of water. As an example, I know of a brewery that makes a hefeweizen and a barleywine with original gravities of 1.047 and 1.091, respectively. The alcohol by volume of each beer is approximately 5 percent and 10 percent. What I intentionally omitted was the final gravity (FG), the reading of the beer's density after fermentation. For you math whizzes, there is a formula to calculate a good approximation of beer's alcohol by volume. It is: OG – FG × 131. Any serious homebrewer will be happy to tell you about the computations.

In summary, the higher the original gravity, the more alcohol in the particular beverage you are drinking.

6

THE DREAM TEAM CASE OF BEER

Let's face it, we love lists. Regardless of the subject, they are fun to analyze, dissect, and critique; then we criticize the author for not including our special favorite. My personal "dream team" case of beer is not necessarily a listing of the twenty-four best beers in the world. The task of defining what makes the "best beer" is itself reason for debate.

The reasons why we drink a certain beer are many. If you are in a bar, socializing with friends, you probably wouldn't be pounding down those brews with a high alcohol content. Rather, you'd opt for something a bit lighter.

If you are planning your meal, then a compatible selection or two might be needed. An cold night before a fire calls for a fuller beer, perhaps something that renders some alcohol warmth. So the ideal beer today may not be the best choice tomorrow.

Nevertheless, I have created a case of beer that should appeal, at least to some degree, to aficionados as well as those who always wanted to see what the "good beer" revolution is all about. No special thought was given to specific places or origin or availability. Keep in mind that most breweries are quite small and do not distribute outside their immediate geographic area. That's why it is essential to check out what is being produced within your region. You may be pleasantly surprised.

In any event, if I could create one remarkable case of beer, this would be it. And that brings up a point worth mentioning. In some states, you cannot buy single bottles of beer, but must purchase larger quantities. Where you live determines where you buy your beer. It may be a grocery store, convenience store, gas station, state-owned business, or privately owned liquor store. Additionally, the specific laws pertaining to the amount of alcohol in beer that can be legally sold vary from state to state. There is more than one state that places a cap on a beer's strength, meaning that there are scores of world-class beers that never have been lawfully sampled there. Do these same restrictions affect other adult beverages? Well, these concerns probably could serve as topics for future books, but I'll save them for a later date.

The twenty-four beers I've selected are among the best of their style. No distinction was given to the place of origin, cost, or distribution. Some may not be available in all regions, but most are. Included with each is the category.

ALASKAN SMOKED PORTER

Porter

In Germany, smoked beers have the name *rauchbier*. The style was practically nonexistent in America until revived by the Alaskan Brewing Company in 1988. Before brewing, the malts are smoked over alder wood, native to the region.

Alaskan Smoked Porter is a seasonal, meaning it is brewed only at a certain time of the year, in this instance autumn. As a porter, its color is dark brown. Don't think the smokiness is all there is in terms of flavor. There is also malt sweetness, and I've detected a slight fruitiness near the end.

As for food pairings, the obvious choices would center on blue cheese and smoked salmon. Other dessert pairings would prove effective, including berries or cheesecake. It is a fine seasoning to sauces, as well.

Smoke serves as a preservative in this beer, and the company projects it to age well. They claim the smoke fades into the background after the first year or two, with flavors of currant, sherry, and raisins emerging in years three or four. By the fifth year, there's a resurfacing of the smoke to the forefront.

Some people have been known to host tastings of differing years of Alaskan Smoked Porter, in an attempt to pinpoint the flavor development, much as with wines. This is known as a vertical tasting.

ANCHOR STEAM

California Common/Steam Beer

You're probably wondering what a California common beer is. You're not alone; so are most people. There are a ton of stories out there as to the beer's origin, but the one that refuses to go away dates back to the time in the nineteenth century when *steam* was a moniker for beer brewed in California without the benefit of cooling. Consequently, there existed no established method for chilling the beer down to lager-style-fermentation temperatures. A brewery would open the roof to expose the beer to the cool air blowing in off the Pacific Ocean. From the outside, you could see a well-defined cloud of steam as it left the building—hence the term *steam*. The term *Steam Beer* is trademarked.

When I was having dinner with former brewery owner Fritz Maytag some time ago, I asked him to confirm the accepted story of how he'd acquired the brewery. In the mid-1960s, Maytag was a graduate student who frequented the Anchor Brewery because he loved the beer. Hearing it was about to close, he purchased 51 percent of it, then bought the remainder a few years later. By the middle of the next decade, he had brewed to capacity and has been successful ever since. I recall hearing Fritz speak to a group of journalists, when he opened his speech by saying, as he held up a bottle of Anchor Steam, "You see this beer? It cost me a million dollars to get it to you today."

Anchor Steam is an American original. It's copper-colored with a rocky white head. There's a balance of toasted malts and citrus from the hops used. No taste sensation is overpowering, in my estimation the sign of a nicely crafted beverage. The alcohol content is only 4.9 percent alcohol by volume (ABV).

If the name *Maytag* sounds familiar, well, it should. Fritz is a part of the company known for home appliances. What few people know is that Fritz is the chairman of the board of Maytag Dairy Farms (ever had Maytag blue cheese?) and the owner of York Creek Vineyards in California.

AVERY THE REVEREND

Quadrupel

In the late 1990s, the late legendary beer writer Michael Jackson spent a couple of days with me touring. On a Tuesday morning, I awoke to find him seated at my kitchen table eating breakfast. I poured myself a cup of coffee and joined him. He said, "Come join me here in an hour or so, I have a beer I want to review with you." It was The Reverend.

A brief history of the beer is worth mentioning. The Reverend is a tribute to the grandfather of Tom Boogaard, Avery's sales manager, an ordained Episcopal minister. The company states, "True to both our 'small brewery, big beers' philosophy and to the spirit and character of the departed Reverend, this beer is strong willed, assertive, and pure of heart, a heart of candy sugar."

The style, Quadrupel, is a very strong abbey-style ale. In the case of The Reverend, double digits are reached (10 percent ABV). You'll taste tiers of fruit, such as cherries and currants, along with a bit of spiciness. Hop presence is negligible. Needless to say, there is an alcohol warmth.

High-octane brews such as this make candidates for maturing. Avery suggests that you can cellar this for up to four years.

AYINGER CELEBRATOR

Doppelbock

The word *bock* is derived from the German town of Einbock, where the style gained recognition. Records of it go back to the early part of the fourteenth century, when the beer enjoyed immense popularity. What many don't realize is that the type actually started at a monastery in northern Italy, but was quickly introduced by Bavarian brewers to compete with bock. Here's a little tip: Doppelbock names end with the suffix *–ator*.

The earliest bocks were bitter, unlike the modern versions. They were brewed in the winter and consequently were housed in chilly conditions, where the lagering (storing) helped smooth out the flavors. *Doppelbock* literally means "double bock," but this is a misnomer. It isn't twice as strong as a regular bock, it's only slightly more intense.

Ayinger Celebrator is thought of as a celebratory beer. It's dark in color and full-bodied from half a year's aging. There's a slight smoky dryness in the finish. But don't mistake the brew; you'll note the fruitiness coming from the malt and whole hop flowers.

Pair this with roast goose, cured ham, smoked duck, turkey, and pastries. A good serving temperature for it is fifty degrees.

BROOKLYN LOCAL 1

Belgian Strong Ale

I had the privilege of first trying this beer at the 2007 Atlantic City Beer Festival, when a company representative gave me a sample of the first iteration of the beer, in comparison with the final product several batches later. Needless to say, the beer that was selected for release is completely different in taste from the original, something not too surprising.

For a new beer to be considered a "must-have" says something about the beverage itself and the brewer, Garrett Oliver. In fact, I understand it cost the company six figures to bring this baby to fruition.

The beer is highly carbonated and reminds me of Duvel (see later in this chapter). I'd recommend a tulip-shaped glass to help capture those champagne-like bubbles. Oliver, himself an accomplished author, employs a process called 100 percent refermentation, meaning the beer goes into the bottle with no carbonation, although added sugar and yeast create the natural effervescence.

The bottling takes place strictly in 750ml bottles, which are both corked and caged. By the way, the bottles were designed in Germany specifically for Local 1.

As for the aroma and taste, there is a potpourri of fruit, including figs, raisins, and plums. The beer is remarkably complex, meaning you'll savor various things at different times, be it the initial sip, the middle, and the aftertaste.

The alcohol content hits 9 percent ABV, so treat this with respect. Local 1 should be a candidate for aging.

CHIMAY GRAND RESERVE (BLUE)

Belgian Dark

Not only does this Trappist abbey produce three types of beer, but they also make exquisite cheeses. Under the supervision of monks who give most of their earnings to help people in need, you'll identify their three beers based on the color of the label.

Chimay Red comes in at 7 percent ABV, Chimay White adds 1 point to that figure, and Blue, also known as Grande Reserve, takes the measurement to 9 percent ABV. All are winners, but Blue probably is considered as the standard, based on its fresh yeasty aroma and roasted malt taste. You can purchase it in 11.2 ounces, 25.4 ounces, or magnum sized at 51 ounces. If you opt for the latter, consider inviting a friend to partake or consider calling in sick at work the next day.

This is a good contender for cellaring, given the proper conditions (away from sunlight, constant cool temperatures, no jostling of the bottle). Be aware of the fact that this beer is bottle-conditioned, meaning you'll find a layer of yeast at the bottom of the bottle. Some people choose to leave an inch or so of the beer in the bottle during the pour; others choose to decant. Personally, I go for the first possibility, but do not discard the small amount left in the bottle. Recognize that that last taste will be different from the initial one based on the accumulation of the yeast.

CZECHVAR

Pilsner

Developed by a Czech brewery dating back to the thirteenth century, this beer has had various names at various times. In North America, it is called Czechvar, but much of the rest of the world refers to it as Budvar or Budweiser. Do you see the problem? So did the courts. In the early part of the twentieth century, it was decided that Anheuser-Busch could use the *Budweiser* name in North America, but Budvar would be called Czechvar. Simple, huh?

In early 2007, the two breweries reached an agreement that permits Anheuser-Busch to serve as the American distributor for Czechvar, a move that has increased availability. There remain, however, disagreements as to the naming of both beers in other countries.

Regardless, Czechvar is a premium lager, aged for no less than ninety days. The foam is thick and golden. There's a good balance between bready malt sweetness and hop bitterness. You may notice a bit of a lemony punch interspersed.

Have one or two . . . or three. These go down really easy.

DOGFISH HEAD MIDAS TOUCH
GOLDEN ELIXIR

Herbal/Spiced

A beer with origins that go back to 700 BC? That's the premise behind Midas Touch, created as a joint effort between the University of

Pennsylvania School of Archaeology and Anthropology and Dogfish Head Brewery. Patrick McGovern, an archaeochemist at the museum, found evidence of an alcoholic beverage that apparently was served at the funerary feast of King Midas, a ruler in central Turkey. Drinking vessels, 157 of them to be exact, were discovered at the site, including a vessel used for serving a beverage at this occurrence. Dr. McGovern learned that the residue within the containers held a "cocktail" consisting of Muscat grape wine, beer from barley, and mead (fermented honey).

Upon his discovery, Sam Calagione, founder of Dogfish Head in nearby Delaware, was commissioned to re-create the drink, based upon findings. Test batches were fashioned and, after some time, Midas Touch was introduced. I was present for the initial tasting, where Calagione, representatives from the museum, and beer expert Michael Jackson explained how the "beer" came to be.

The bottling line at the Delaware-based Dogfish Head, arguably one of the most celebrated American breweries. Dogfish Head has gained a reputation for developing unusual, but flavorful beers and has gained a following extending beyond the U.S. border.

Identifying the drink was the initial problem. Was it wine, mead, or beer? Because it is fermented, it is classified as a beer, although drinking it (9 percent ABV) might give you reason for doubt. If you concentrate on it and your sense of taste is at its peak, you'll detect elements of all three. There is a definite grape presence as well as sweetness from honey, merging with grain. Oh, and saffron—a remarkably expensive spice derived from the saffron crocus flower—is in the recipe as a slight bittering agent. It may have been used prior to the discovery of hops. Ask a chef about its cost and you'll learn that it easily can run up to sixty-five dollars for a single ounce.

Calagione compares Midas Touch to Chardonnay; Jackson likens it to champagne and suggests serving it in a fluted glass. It's not the sort of drink you'd want to drink over and over, but for a completely unique treat, this is one well worth your search.

DUVEL

Belgian Strong Pale

The first time I tried this beer, I thought I had reached nirvana. What impressed me initially was the billowy layer of white foam atop a golden, highly carbonated liquid. My first sip confirmed my hopes; this was a classic and would join my Hall of Fame. It weighs in at over 8 percent ABV, so don't get mesmerized by the enticing light color. And those bubbles never seem to go away.

As for the taste, well, you'll note a host of sensations. The malt sweetness never really dissipates, but lingers delicately while you get waves of bread yeast, hop bitterness, and alcohol warmth as you swallow.

Do be careful in your initial pour. The company recommends their own glassware, of course, but a widemouthed tulip will do. Angle the glass as you pour slowly along its side. Stop when you get about two-thirds of the way filled, as that enormous head will take over.

The meaning of the word *Duvel*? It's "devil" in Flemish. And that's because it is a devil of a good beer.

KONA LONGBOARD LAGER

American Lager

I first became acquainted with this Hawaiian brewery not long after they opened in 1995. At the time, I received a bottle of a limited-edition beer and fell in love with it and the company. Longboard Lager, first released in 1998, is fermented and aged for five weeks and has a subtle, spicy hop aroma that balances the maltiness you might expect from an all-grain lager.

You might refer to this as a "session beer," meaning that it is satisfying enough to have a few. That's not something you might do with those big beers that approach double digits in alcohol. Longboard Lager weighs in at 5.5 percent ABV. There's a slight bit of wheat in the recipe, giving it a creaminess. The finish is dry and filling.

Longboard Lager should prove to be fairly flexible when it comes to food pairings. Light dishes will work, but so will some heartier foods, such as pizza or chicken.

LINDEMANS FRAMBOISE

Fruit Lambic

If there ever was a beer designed for dessert, this is it. I recall once hosting a combination beer/wine dinner at an elegant restaurant located near Atlantic City. I worked with a wine expert in pairing the beverages for the evening. A couple of weeks prior to the dinner, we met at the restaurant. The entire meal was served to us to help us to determine which drinks to choose. Although we talked about the food and drink possibilities, neither of us tipped our hands as to what we might offer for the diners to drink. As it turns out, the chocolate-based dessert was matched with Lindemans Framboise, meaning "raspberry," and the wine critic selected a raspberry wine. When the two beverages were served, the only way to tell them apart was the slight head on the beer.

The customers voted as to which drinks created a better match and Lindemans won by a three-to-one margin. It's worth mentioning that the majority of clients that evening were wine drinkers. Hey, why preach to the choir?

The brewery is located in the Flanders region of Belgium, where lambics are well known and appreciated. The Lindemans Farm Brewery probably is the yardstick for producers using spontaneous fermentation—a process by which wild yeast from Belgium's Seine River Valley ferments locally grown barley and wheat (the percentage of barley is 70 percent, with wheat making up the remaining 30 percent). Aged hops are used because bitterness is not a trait that is sought. After the beer is aged in oak barrels, fresh fruit is added, generating a secondary fermentation.

As I mentioned, a pairing with a chocolate dessert is unbeatable, but I've also drizzled a bit of it over a dish of sorbet. The alcohol content is only 4 percent ABV. If you like this flavor, try some of their others, including *kriek* (black cherry), *pêche* (peach), *cassis* (black currant), and gueuze (traditional).

MELBOURN BROTHERS STRAWBERRY

Fruit Beer

This British brewery had faced its share of problems in its close-to-two-hundred-year history. A fire in 1876 destroyed the facility, causing it to be rebuilt. In the 1970s, it was felt that the plant simply had outlived its usefulness. The bulk of its customers came from the pubs in the Stamford area. Fortunately, the company reorganized itself by 1994, when a return to time-honored brewing traditions was embraced. Fresh fruit became the seasoning, a throwback to the days before hops were used both as a spice and a preservative.

There are similarities in production between all the Melbourn Brothers products (which include apricot and cherry as well as strawberry) and Lindemans. Both are spontaneously fermented, both use fruit, and both pair fabulously with desserts or certain cheeses. Yet there are noticeable differences between the two drinks. Flavors of sweet and tart balance each other, and they go down far too easily. Thank goodness there's less than 4 percent ABV in each bottle, because folks tend to drink them like soda.

Be aware that these beers aren't the easiest to obtain and can be very costly. You'll probably buy them as singles. I highly recommend trying all three flavors at some point.

ORVAL

Belgian Pale Ale

If you've gotten the impression that I love Belgian ales, you are on target. Brewed and bottled at the Orval monastery founded in the eleventh century, this beer's unique flavor comes from triple fermentation using three different malts, two types of hops, and two strains of yeast.

The beer is orange in color, and you'll take in a lemony aroma and a tart, dry flavor. As with many beers of this ilk, foam retention is extraordinary. The concentrated carbonation creates the impression that this is a bigger beer than it really is. In fact, the alcohol level is just 5.4 percent ABV.

I like drinking this out of a chalice (Orval makes a beautiful gold-lined one). Beers that are fragrant and bubbly reach their peak in containers such as this. It also is visually quite appealing.

By the way, look for what is known as "Belgian lace" as you are drinking Orval—a distinctive pattern of bubbles that cling to the sides of the glass as you drink.

Check out the shape of the Orval bottle, introduced in 1929 and described as "skittle" or pin-shaped.

The brewery recommends pairing Orval with bread, fresh pears, steamed mussels, clams, oysters, smoked salmon, and trout. Cellaring is favored; the company feels the beer will be good for up to five years. With a beer as good as Orval, do you really want to wait that long?

RODENBACH GRAND CRU

Flemish Sour Ale

This may be one of the most atypical styles of beer you'll ever encounter. It is a derivation of Rodenbach Original, which is a blend of new and aged ales. Grand Cru is the matured quantity. By now, you may be wondering if this isn't just a ploy to pawn off old beer on the consumer. Nothing could be farther from the truth. Grand Cru gets its sharpness and sourness from aging the beer for up to two years in oak barrels. The remaining bacteria in those barrels impart the acidity in this beer. The slight level of fruit can lead drinkers to believe the beer is a red wine; it is not uncommon for Grand Cru to be a special favorite of wine connoisseurs.

Alcohol content is moderate (6 percent ABV). Not surprisingly, there is no noticeable hop presence. I've been in the presence of those who love Rodenbach Grand Cru despite professing to not liking the taste of beer. Then again, this is hardly what one might expect from a "traditional" beer.

ROGUE SHAKESPEARE STOUT

American Stout

A distinctive brewery, to say the least, based in Oregon. They've carved a niche for themselves by doing some experimental brews, most of which hit the mark.

What makes an American stout, as opposed to the Irish type? Look no farther than the recipe. Rogue Shakespeare Stout's is distinctly American and includes the citrusy Cascade hop.

The beer pours black in color and develops a creamy head. Because of the use of chocolate malt, you'll get a chocolate aftertaste.

Note the following. Porters and stouts tend to feel "chewy" as you drink them, meaning there is substance to the brews. Think about the experience of eating a peanut butter and jelly sandwich: The peanut butter feels thicker than the jelly. In beertalk, that's called mouthfeel. Porters and stouts have more mouthfeel than light domestic lagers, for example, which nothing to do with the amount of alcohol in each. In the case of Shakespeare Stout, we're talking about 6 percent ABV.

Some people like blending this beer with another of Rogue's specialties, their Dead Guy Ale, creating a concoction playfully referred to as a Dead Poet.

SAISON DUPONT

Saison

Ask five experts to describe a saison and you probably will get five different answers. Literally, *saison* is the French word for "season," and that might explain the origin of the style. In history, these were working-class beers, produced at a farmhouse. They were brewed in the winter, prior to refrigeration, then aged until consumption the following summer. Saisons had a low alcohol content, perhaps in the 3 to 4 percent range, because they were designed for hydration—back then, much of the drinking water available simply was not potable. And let's face it, we know what happens to one's ability to work once too much alcohol has been consumed. Today's versions, however, have about twice the alcohol.

Eventually saisons reached a point of near-extinction, but their popularity has reawakened in the United States, leading to an appreciation of those from northern France and Belgium. In the case of Saison Dupont, the home is Wallonia, a French-speaking section of Belgium. And it truly is a working farm; you can buy eggs there as well as beer.

If you're among the uninitiated, the smell of a saison could be enough to lead you to think it had spoiled. Saison Dupont is earthy and yeasty. You might take in a musty straw aroma. Uninviting traits to some, but most desirable in beers of this type.

As you pour, you'll notice that the beer is cloudy, because it's unfiltered. Don't be afraid; it's nothing more than yeast, which is high in B vitamins. Filtration would remove much of the flavor, which is tart, somewhat fruity, spicy, and bread-like. Intricate to say the least.

One national American magazine named Saison Dupont as the best beer in the world. I don't know if it is, but it's certainly one I wouldn't want to go without for long.

SAMUEL ADAMS CHOCOLATE BOCK

Bock

Beer for dessert? Is nothing sacred? Chocolate Bock originally was brewed to celebrate Valentine's Day a few years ago, but it was a huge hit—all fifty thousand bottles sold out. What separates this beer from most others is how it's made. It is a bock, meaning it's a lager that lifts weights, with a fuller malt sweetness and dark color.

Ah, here is where it gets interesting. The Scharffen Berger chocolate company created a blend of chocolate for the Boston Beer Company (the actual name of the brewery). The beer aged on a bed of "nibs," the center of the chocolate bean, rendering a rich flavor to the beverage. There's a bit of vanilla added to hold it all together.

The packaging is hip. The label on the 750ml bottle—the only size in which this beer is packaged—is pewter.

Is this the sort of beer you'd want to guzzle? Hardly. It does, however, team up well with chocolate desserts, cheesecake, and fruit. I've taken a scoop of vanilla ice cream and filled the glassware with Chocolate Bock, making one heck of a float.

SAMUEL ADAMS UTOPIAS

Strong Ale

Name the beverage that matches the following characteristics: It's 27 percent ABV (that's 54 proof), it's served in a brandy snifter in two-ounce increments, it should be consumed at room temperature, it's "still" (not carbonated), a bottle of it retails for over a hundred dollars, some have sold for several hundred dollars, various types of yeast are used including a variety found in champagne, only a few thousand bottles are produced, and it tastes like a fine cognac, sherry, or vintage port.

Probably the last response you'd give here is beer. Yet that is exactly what Utopias is, falling into a relatively new class of beers under the banner of "extreme": brews with an extremely high alcohol content that also use nontraditional brewing ingredients.

Even the "bottle" of Utopias is nontraditional. It resembles the copper kettle used by brewers for so many years.

It speaks volumes for the beer-buying industry that, given the popularity of low-alcohol beers, the market for extreme beers is powerful. Granted, they (including Utopias) aren't for everyone, but if you are ready to go to the last level in beer tasting, Utopias is the Utopia.

SAMUEL SMITH'S NUT BROWN ALE

English Brown Ale

Coming from Yorkshire's oldest brewery, founded in 1758, this beer's attraction stems in part from its water source. The brewing water is high in natural minerals and is drawn from the original well sunk over two hundred years ago. The yeast strain has remained unchanged since the beginning of the last century.

The fermenting system of Nut Brown is known as "Yorkshire Square." Trying to summarize it in a limited amount of space is difficult, but think of it as a two-leveled process in which the cooling beer is fermented on the lower compartment while the yeast rises to an upper chamber. Sporadically, the beer from the bottom is pumped up to the yeasty head, then is allowed to settle and cool at the bottom.

Brown ale is one of England's oldest styles of beer and has been mentioned in literature as far back as the sixteenth century. Samuel Smith's has a walnut color and a taste of hazelnuts tempered with aromatic hops. This is a beer I recommend for those who are in transition from drinking strictly light-colored brews, but are afraid of porters or stouts. Consider matching this with a barbecued dish, Chinese food, and certain cheeses. The alcohol content is 5 percent ABV.

SCHNEIDER WEISSE

Hefeweizen

A Hefeweizen is a German wheat beer that is unfiltered. When you look at it, it will appear cloudy. As we've seen previously, this is nothing more than yeast. The prefix *hefe* is German for "yeast." *Weizen* or *weisse* signifies a white beer, or a wheat-based beverage. The amount of wheat can fluctuate, but up to 50 percent wheat or higher is not uncommon. Wheat is light and refreshing, a nice warm-weather drink. Another aspect of wheat beers is creaminess. When you're pouring one into a glass, do so slowly or risk having it run over the rim. Head retention is great. Hey, this is a cool-looking beer!

I love serving this at a tasting, especially to those who never have had a hefeweizen. The beer is redolent of cloves, bananas, nutmeg, and pepper. Take your first sip and notice how those fragrances carry over into the taste.

At some pubs, the server may ask if you want a wedge of lemon added. I recommend you try it without. The lemon cuts the yeastiness, but it also adulterates the flavor as intended by the brewer. If aesthetics are important, know that the acid from the fruit cuts through the layer of foam like a hot knife through butter.

SIERRA NEVADA PALE ALE

American Pale Ale

One of the original players in the microbrew revolution, Sierra Nevada started back in 1980 in Chico, California. Since then, their pale ale has become recognized as the benchmark for American pale ales. Open the bottle and pour a few ounces. Get a whiff of the aroma and take your first sip. That biting, citrus feel you get is what makes this an American take on a British style of beer. Cascade hops are employed, a favorite of the new breed of brewers, especially on the West Coast. Despite their popularity, though, these hopes are still seldom used to any degree by major breweries.

I once visited a new brewery that was developing its American pale ale and was privy to tasting various trials of it as it was being refined. When I asked the lead brewer if he had a flavor profile in mind, I recall him saying that he was molding his beer to replicate that of Sierra Nevada.

Beers that go overboard with hops tend to be one-dimensional. Sierra Nevada's adaptation has a definite hop presence, but the malt crispness is what makes this so special. Lingering sugars will come out near the finish, and the beer ends delightfully dry.

The beer is bottle-conditioned, in theory implying that it may have a prolonged shelf life. But hops lose a lot over time. My experience has been to drink this beer as fresh as possible and not worry about cellaring.

I'd match this with spicy dishes and salads. Hoppy beers tend to stimulate the appetite, so many choose to start off a meal with this brew. Alcohol content is 5.6 percent ABV.

STONE ARROGANT BASTARD ALE

American Strong Ale

Stone Brewing's promotion for this beer says a lot: "This is an aggressive beer. You probably won't like it. It is quite doubtful that you have the taste or sophistication to be able to appreciate an ale of this quality and depth. We would suggest that you stick to safer and more familiar territory . . ."

The beer is a reddish brown and extremely fragrant. At your first sip, you'll get a blast of malt sweetness coupled with caramel and roasted flavors. Then the alcohol kicks in (it reaches 7.2 percent ABV). Finally, you'll get a blast of hops, but it helps to balance the initial sensation. I really appreciate complexity in a beer, as opposed to so many of those one-dimensional brews.

Along with beers from companies like Anchor and Sierra Nevada, Stone Brewing's beverages typify the notion that West Coast beers are inimitable. If you like Arrogant Bastard, check out their Oaked Arrogant Bastard, aged in oak chips. This features a bit more complexity with the addition of a vanilla, woody aroma, and flavor.

UNIBROUE LA FIN DU MONDE

Belgian Strong Pale Ale

Coming from Quebec's remarkable Unibroue, La Fin du Monde weighs in at 9 percent alcohol by volume (ABV), but that level is amazingly masked by the complexity of the beverage. Golden, with a never-ending layer of foam, this beer offers waves of spice, fruit, and hops.

This beer first came out in 1994 after eighteen month of research. The beer's name translates to "the End of the World," a reference in honor of explorers who had thought they had reached the end of the world when they had discovered America.

This is another high-octane beer. The company says you can age this for eight years or more, but why wait?

WESTMALLE TRAPPIST

Tripel

The Westmalle Abbey, located north of Antwerp, Belgium, is one of only seven Trappist breweries in the world. Founded near the end of the eighteenth century, the brewery is recognized for having defined the dubbel (or double) and tripel (or triple) styles. There are misconceptions surrounding these types of beers. Some believe a Dubbel to be twice the strength of a "regular" beer and a tripel to be three times the potency. In reality, a dubbel generally has an alcohol by volume content of about 6.5 to 7.0 percent, and a tripel approaches 9.0 percent.

The color of each type varies also. Dubbels are dark amber; tripels commonly are golden. This flies in the face of the belief that dark-colored beers contain more alcohol. Why the color variation? Tripels use a pilsner malt and added white candy sugar.

As for Westmalle Tripel, you'll note the malt sweetness coupled with an herbal aroma that increases as the beer warms a bit. I find it remarkably flexible and have had this beer as an accompaniment to my main dish or with various cheeses.

7

CONCLUSION

Check out a listing of the best-selling American beers and you'll notice a common theme. Virtually all look and taste the same. The inventory includes items such as Bud Light, Miller Lite, Budweiser, Busch Light, Coors Light, Corona, and Heineken. Each beer is golden in color, fizzy, and lacking in abundant flavor. Although my personal bias probably is evident, I cannot deny that these beers are doing something very right. They dominate the American scene and apparently offer what the majority of drinkers desire. The ubiquity of these brands hardly makes them bad beers; indeed, they are expertly constructed. A Budweiser in Los Angeles tastes precisely the same as one consumed in Detroit and another purchased in Atlanta. Consistency has been perfected, and there is comfort in using products that offer reliability. Hey, if you're a fan of these beers, you shouldn't be criticized or feel guilty for not being a part of the revolution in the industry. At least once a week, someone approaches me almost apologetic for admitting a liking of a mass-marketed beer. You don't have to explain your choices to anyone. My purpose is to attempt to introduce you to some of the newer options on hand and provide choices. Remember that many of the very small breweries in this country operate on a shoestring budget and don't advertise. They rely on information circulated via some of the means mentioned previously, such as "beeriodicals," websites, and festivals to get the word out. I've heard it said that companies like Anheuser-Busch probably spill more beer in one day than most microbreweries produce in a year.

What's been happening in the beer industry now is a natural growth from the birth of the craft-brewing scene in the late 1970s. I actually had gotten away from drinking much beer at that time. I just felt that either the sector or I was in a rut. It was kind of like that old Peggy Lee song, "Is That All There Is?" I experimented with other beverages, but kept coming back to my drink of choice, just in lesser amounts.

My epiphany occurred in Washington, DC, when an acquaintance brought me to a place called The Brickskeller, lovingly described as a "hole in the wall." More beautiful words could not be spoken. This absolutely mesmerizing establishment featured over a thousand different beers from around the world. You could buy anything from Louisiana's Abita Amber to Poland's Zywiec, with plenty in between. And yes, they even sold Budweiser. I remember walking through that place, looking at the overabundance of beer bottles—brands that neither of us had heard of—wondering what I had stumbled into. My friend became my guru, and he was about to take me on my first psychedelic experience.

I think I drank a Grolsch at the time because everything else seemed so bizarre to me. As I sipped that first beer, I couldn't help but wonder if beers like these would become the impetus for massive change. Little did I know what an understatement that would turn out to be!

I became so turned on by the explosion of flavors that I started buying beers from companies that were unfamiliar to me. If I liked the label art or if the brewery had a distinct name, I tried it. It was a throwback to the times when I would buy an album (remember those?) because of the band name or the artwork.

In time, I became enthralled by stories of the creation of these very small breweries, many times run as single-person operations. There are accounts from all over the country, all around the world, actually, of people who invested in a dream. As an example, let's look at little Harlem Brewing Company of New York.

Celeste Beatty, a saxophonist, had a long-standing interest in beer and had actively been homebrewing for a few years. Her interest in the craft led her to start a brewery, after preparing numerous test batches. Because the name for her initial brew would be critical, research was done and focus groups were established to evaluate her beverage. The Sugar Hill district, in the extreme northern part of Manhattan, was home to such notables as Cab Calloway and Duke Ellington, who in his signature song "Take the 'A' Train (To Sugar Hill)" was describing an affluent neighborhood. Although some people associated the area with the Sugarhill Gang, a hip-hop group who gained national recognition in 1979, "most reflected on the legacy and history of Duke Ellington and all the greats of the day," according to Ms. Beatty. With that, Sugar Hill Golden Ale was born and a distribution contract was signed.

Accounts like this are everywhere, and it is this sort of thing that is driving the beer business. Not every company will achieve financial success; many will fail. Yet there is no mistaking that fact that this is a wonderful time to be a lover of this remarkable beverage.

QUICK RESOURCES

In this age of rapid information retrieval, folks love to gather as much knowledge on a subject as possible, assuming it comes from reliable sources. Worldwide, well over one billion people are using the Internet. In North America, 70 percent of the population draws on electronic media for various activities. As it applies to the subject of beer, 'Net research is flourishing with no sign of a letup.

So let's identify where you might go to get the essentials on this beverage. Needless to say, if you are interested in the most current information, then do access the Internet. One of the best sources is Beer Advocate (www.beeradvocate.com). There are sections dealing with festivals, news, styles, events, and a forum where members may exchange ideas. I find the reviews to be exceptional, including those by brothers Jason and Todd Alstrom, creators and moderators of the site, as well as by the many regulars who frequently post. I've not identified any biases in terms of product favorites; the site seems to be quite impartial. I'd make this my first choice for reference.

California-based Jay Brooks runs the Brookston Beer Bulletin (www.brookstonbeerbulletin.com), a particularly instructive site complete with reviews and candid opinions. You think Jay likes his beer? He has a son named Porter. You'll like the fact that Jay constantly updates his blog. I'd bookmark this and check it on a daily basis.

Don Russell is an award-winning author and columnist known to many as Joe Sixpack. In fact, his website is www.joesixpack.net. Don't let his moniker fool you; he's craft-beer-savvy. His first book, *Joe Sixpack's Philly Beer Guide,* should be considered a must for anyone visiting the City of Brotherly Love. Philadelphia has some notable watering holes, and Russell identifies them for you, complete with a walking tour map. Maybe it should be called a stumbling tour.

Realbeer.com (www.realbeer.com) is another terrific source on an assortment of beer topics, including how to brew, beer and health, and much more. The site features columns by some of the top writers around the world, giving Realbeer.com a global focus.

I got to know Canadian Stephen Beaumont several years ago when we toured a few breweries. I consider him one of the most knowledgeable people around on the subject of beer and food pairings. Beaumont has written for many of the top newspapers and magazines in the world and has authored several books, including *Premium Beer Drinker's Guide*. Not too long ago, he opened beerbistro, a very beer-friendly dining establishment in Toronto. Check out its site at www.beerbistro.com for an understanding of Beaumont's philosophy.

Stephen publishes a website called World of Beer at www.worldofbeer.com with monthly tasting reviews and updates. Get on his mailing list to receive his latest announcements.

If you have an interest in homebrewing, Brew Your Own, a spin-off of the magazine of the same name, is an exceptional site. Actually, you don't have to be a homebrewer to get value from BYO. Visiting the website at www.byo.com will give you a greater understanding of the beer you are drinking. They profile beer styles and delve into related beverages, such as mead.

If you enjoy Brew Your Own, you should find value in Modern Brewery Age (www.breweryage.com). Though pitched to people working in the beverage trade, the site and magazine have kept pace with the times and emphasize the craft and imported beer segments, as well as upcoming trends.

The Beer Institute started in the 1980s to lobby Congress on behalf of beer industry. Members include a comprehensive cross section of the largest breweries in the United States, in addition to the smallest of micros. Adjunct businesses also are members. For the consumer, there are sections pertaining to beer history, and the links section is noteworthy.

The Brewers Association (www.beertown.org) was set up to advance US craft-brewing interests. There are informative links on the website to such topics as "Beer and Health" and "Beer and Food." Information is informative and easy to read. The site is regularly updated, with facts and figures kept as timely as possible.

In the late 1980s, "brewspapers," or beer-themed newspapers, entered the scene. *Celebrator Beer News* was the first to make a national impact; it still exists today, stronger than ever. The publication is a bi-monthly and is available through subscription. There is a distinct West Coast focus to *Celebrator,* but recent years have seen the addition of writers from other locales. I especially like the fact that they employ top-notch journalists, including the aforementioned Jay Brooks and Steve Beaumont, Jack Curtin, Lisa Morrison, Carolyn Smagalksi, Christina Perozzi, and Fred Eckhardt.

Ale Street News started in 1992 in the northern part of New Jersey and quickly gained a loyal following. Whereas *Celebrator* had a West Coast feel, *ASN* garnered a market on the East Coast. That has changed in recent years to more of a national and international market, but the quality and relevance have not. Circulation is near the hundred-thousand mark, making it the most widely "beeriodical" in the United States.

Brewing News, like *Celebrator* and *Ale Street,* is a bi-monthly. Unlike the others, *Brewing News* is a series of regional newspapers, ensuring excellent local coverage. There currently are seven such periodicals under the company umbrella: *Great Lakes Brewing News, Southwest Brewing News, Mid-Atlantic Brewing News, Yankee Brew News, Northwest Brewing News, Rocky Mountain Brewing News,* and *Southern Brew News.* Certain featured articles may be repeated in all publications, but the individual writers live within the area they serve.

The "Big Three" newspapers of the industry can be had via subscription for approximately twenty dollars each per year, but you may also be able to obtain them for free. Many well-stocked purveyors of beer and most breweries and brewpubs offer them to their public just for visiting. You probably won't find *Celebrator* in Boston, nor will

Yankee Brew News be available in San Francisco, but the odds of finding at least one of these publications are good. In my area, I regularly pick up *Ale Street News* and *Mid-Atlantic Brewing News* and haven't paid for a copy in years.

As I stated, there is no place where you'll find timelier information than online. Use your favorite browser to conduct a search and you'll find scores of pertinent sites, offering anything you might want to know. Do recognize that this medium is volatile and that sites can and do change regularly. I have a high degree of confidence that those websites documented here will remain intact for some time.

The rise in online programming is supplanting that of more traditional means, such as commercial television. Sources such as YouTube, iTunes, Viddler, and many more allow visitors literally thousands of programming choices. Unfortunately, today's favorite could easily be gone tomorrow. Recommending specific programming is meaningless for exactly that reason. Still, I'm relatively confident that original shows on the subject of beer will continue to be developed for the foreseeable future. They certainly are worth checking out, and most are totally free.

INDEX